THE PELICAN GUIDE TO
Louisiana

Longue Vue Gardens, New Orleans. (Courtesy Louisiana Office of Tourism)

THE PELICAN GUIDE TO

Louisiana

SECOND EDITION

Mary Ann Sternberg

PELICAN PUBLISHING COMPANY
Gretna 1993

First edition, 1989
Second edition, 1993

*The word "Pelican" and the depiction of a pelican are trademarks
of Pelican Publishing Company, Inc., and are registered
in the U.S. Patent and Trademark Office.*

Library of Congress Cataloging-in-Publication Data

Sternberg, Mary Ann.
    The Pelican guide to Louisiana / Mary Ann Sternberg.—2nd ed.
    p.   cm.
    Includes index.
    ISBN 0-88289-901-5
    1. Louisiana—Guidebooks.   I. Title.
F367.3.S74 1993
917.6304'63—dc20   92-39301
                                                                CIP

Information in this guidebook is based on authoritative data available at the
time of printing. Hours of operation of offices and attractions listed are subject to change without notice. Readers are asked to take this into account when
consulting this guide.

*Cover photo credits: Top right, Layton Castle, courtesy Monroe-West Monroe Conven-
tion and Visitors Bureau; others courtesy of Louisiana Office of Tourism*

Manufactured in the United States of America
Published by Pelican Publishing Company, Inc.
1101 Monroe Street, Gretna, Louisiana 70053

Contents

Acknowledgments

Compiling this kind of book entailed great cooperation from many sources; so did revising it. My sincerest appreciation and warmest thanks go to the following who helped in a variety of ways:

June Carter and her staff at the Office of Tourism's regional headquarters in Greenwood who compiled the 1984 *River Trails, Bayous and Back Roads* for the Office of Tourism, which served as an inspiration and a model for this book.

To the State Office of Tourism, especially Bruce Morgan and Pat Guercio.

To the staffs of the visitors and convention bureaus all over the state, tourist information agencies, chambers of commerce, departments of economic development and all those interested enough in the attractions of their area to willingly talk with me and help with this update.

To my Unique Louisiana experts: Raymond Cedotal, W. H. Taylor, Jr., Betty Anne Eaves, Jacques Michel, and Capt. B. M. Cathcart, The Louisiana Association of Museums, Jean Lafitte National Park Service, Debbie Woodiel, Dennis LaBat, Ernest Landry, Paul Tate, Jr., Lucy Parlange, Dale Lauter, Will Peck, Glen Salter, Patty Gay.

To my children for their patience, their indulgence and their love.

To my mother, for her input on New Orleans. And to Josef, from whose memory I continue to receive inspiration.

Confederate soldier statue in front of the Claiborne Parish Courthouse, Homer. (Courtesy Louisiana Office of Tourism)

Introduction

If one of my weaknesses is travel, I also confess to an unfocused set of interests, an attitude verging on perpetual wonder about the world and the desire to share my observations. Add to this the lucky happenstance of living in a fascinating place and you've got the recipe for *The Pelican Guide to Louisiana*.

When I set out to compile a tour guide to the state, my motivation was derived from love of the place as I knew it—as a life-long resident of New Orleans and Baton Rouge and as an explorer of both legendary tourist centers and of certain wonderful other nooks and crannies that offered lovely surprises. The incredible diversity of the state is delightful to visitors as well as to us who live here.

But my research for this book amazed me! I uncovered much, much more than I had ever imagined . . . from tiny rural museums and restored, 19th century, handhewn log cabins, picturesque trails, and splendid scenery, to one-of-a-kind places like Pilot Town, significant sites like Marksville, and sophisticated collections of art and treasure. I discovered that Louisiana is a cultural cornucopia, an impressive array of entertainment and recreational facilities, of every conceivable form of arts—from fine art to folklife, and a geography boasting not only a rich and varied history but also an exciting mix of habitats and treasures of flora and fauna. With the possible exception of mountains, it offers almost anything one could want.

The best format for presenting this trove of information on what to see and do in Louisiana seemed to be through using short, paragraph-style entries, arranged geographically, to give a brief, hopefully useful, description of the attractions. But certain subjects demanded fuller treatment, a more personal, more impressionistic response. These are the subjects of the twelve spirit-of-place essays that reflect my personal experience overlaid onto background research.

Through these longer descriptions I've tried to convey what makes their subjects unique or interesting. A few are quite familiar, such as the St. Charles Avenue Streetcar, now the longest continually operating line in the country; others are lesser known, such as the Catahoula Hound, Louisiana's native dog, and the sawmill village of Fisher. These essays represent the only subjective matter in an otherwise objective text.

Dividing a state tour guide into chapters requires making arbitrary decisions. We have chosen to use accepted geographic or economic divisions of the state already in place, with hub cities surrounded by mutually interested parishes. Nevertheless, in some cases, chapter boundaries seem capricious. Related, probably contiguous, areas may appear in other sections. Because of such proscriptions, I advise readers to look at the state map to find what else is nearby, or on the way to where you're going, or perhaps just a little farther on. I have, in fact, reordered two of the divisions for this second edition for this reason.

Naturally, the special flavor and color of any region is best discovered where the locals gather, "off the beaten track," even beyond the established, well-publicized attractions. It's well worth seeking. And though I've tried to include some of the myriad of interesting, local entertainments, you can enhance the list immensely by asking the visitors' information centers and by reading local daily or weekly newspapers. I have also included references to the arts councils in each area which can furnish reliable, up-to-date details about special museum exhibits, performances of music, dance or theatre, lectures, and other events.

Attractions included in this guide are considered open and public if their regular hours of operation are listed; by appointment ("by appt."), for which you must call to arrange a time to visit; and drive-by, which indicates that the attraction (often an historic home) is private and **not** open to the public, yet, because of its architecture, atmosphere, landscape, or history, is worth a glimpse from the exterior. Admission, of course, means that a fee is charged.

In any extensive tour guide, some very worthwhile attractions are inadvertently excluded or details may be incorrect. Worse still, some places may have closed or changed their operation dramatically since the information was compiled. For this reason, I encourage you to check specific attractions before travelling a great distance to see them. For an afternoon of meandering, however, it may be more fun to just go. And as for those inevitable omissions, I urge you to write me in care of the publisher so that they may be considered for inclusion in future revisions of the guide. I am grateful to several readers who did so after the publication of the first edition, which enabled me to make this second edition of the guide more comprehensive.

Seeing Louisiana and its attractions, understanding its character and personality, and wandering its byways are activities for an hour, a weekend, or a lifetime. So whether you're just visiting or wanting to see more of the state you live in, I can offer just one word of advice:

Enjoy!

Nottoway Plantation Home, White Castle. (Courtesy Louisiana Office of Tourism)

THE PELICAN GUIDE TO
Louisiana

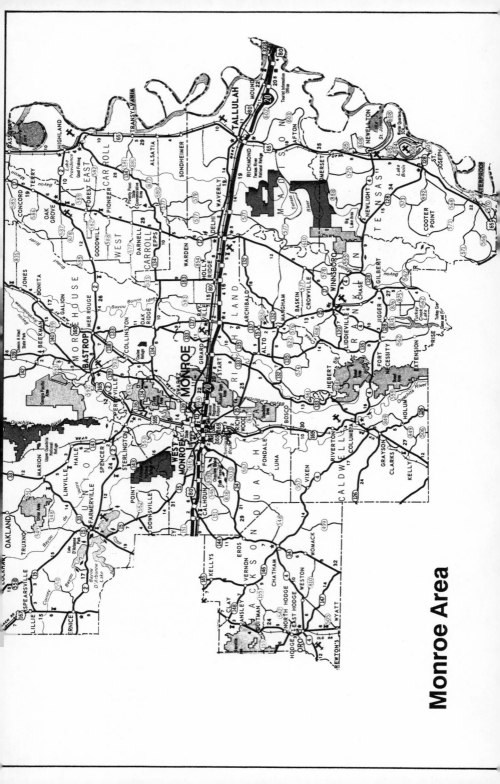

Monroe Area

1

Monroe and the Northeast

Union, Morehouse, East Carroll, West Carroll, Madison, Richland, Ouachita, Caldwell, Franklin, Tensas, and Jackson parishes comprise the northeast section of the state. Known by the original Indians as Ouachita (pronounced Wah-sha-taw), the Land of the Sacred Silver Waters, northeast Louisiana was first settled by Protestant Anglo-Saxons, part of the westward expansion from the original colonies. Cotton was the original economic mainstay, and plantation houses abounded, though many were burned during the Civil War. The area is well known for fishing and hunting. Monroe is the largest city in northeast Louisiana.

BERNICE, surrounded by timber and farmland, was settled by families from Tennessee, Kentucky, Alabama, and Georgia. **The Alabama Methodist Church** (off Alt. La. 2), built circa 1895, is a good example of early country churches. **The Corney Creek Festival** and **Governor's Cup Canoe Races** (first weekend in June) have old-fashioned contests, parades, and games. (318-285-9071).

LAKE D'ARBONNE STATE PARK, west of Farmerville off La. 2, is 600 acres of wooded recreation area and includes fishing, cabins, boat dock, and camping. Fees. (318-368-8322)

FARMERVILLE, named for William W. Farmer, lieutenant governor during the years 1852-53, hosts the annual Watermelon Festival (last weekend in July). Edgewood, constructed in 1902, is the most extravagant example of Queen Anne architecture in the region. Private. (318-368-9242 for information on scheduled house tours.)

PHILLIPS LAKE, between Farmerville and Sterlington off La. 2, is a small cypress-shaded, freshwater lake that is part of Bayou de L'Outre. Fishing. Boat launch.

BAYOU DE L'OUTRE NATURE TRAIL, designated a National Scenic River from Arkansas until it joins the Ouachita River near Sterlington. Heavily wooded, some swamp. Guide recommended.

UNION WILDLIFE MANAGEMENT AREA, off La. 33, is a tract of over 12,000 acres of pine and hardwood forest, spring-fed streams, and good birdwatching. Hunting and trapping by permit. Primitive camping. (318-343-4044)

MARION: Hopkins House, circa 1850, on Hopkins Lane, is a white, frame, two-story showplace; the only Bluffland plantation home in the area. Open by appointment. Annual spring pilgrimage of homes. **Mayhaw Festival** held the last weekend in May.

GEORGIA PACIFIC WILDLIFE MANAGEMENT AREA: five miles northwest of Bastrop, this 27,000-acre tract has excellent hunting in season, trapping by permit, bird-watching. Campsites nearby, but not onsite. (318-343-4044)

BUSSEY BRAKE: this 2,000-acre man-made reservoir north of Bastrop is a renowned fishing spot, famous for large bass and catfish. Camping and boat rental available.

CHEMIN-A-HAUT STATE PARK: the name means "high road" in French. Located east of La. 139, 10 miles north of Bastrop on Bayou Bartholomew, this 405-acre park is a portion of the high road to the south once used by the Indians in their seasonal migrations. Boating, cabins, camping, swimming, and trails. (318-281-5805)

UPPER OUACHITA NATIONAL WILDLIFE REFUGE: a 21,000-acre recreation area with fishing and hunting (in season). Lake Finch offers fishing, scenic area, boat launch, and rentals. Hunting permits sold. (318-325-1735)

BASTROP: laid out in 1846 by the Baron de Bastrop along the banks of Bayou Bartholemew. **The Snyder Museum,** located on La. 165 north on the Mer Rouge Road, features historic documents, 18th and 19th century furnishings, china, kitchen utensils, and other collections, as well as special exhibits. The grounds include gardens and picnic facilities. Open Mon.-Fri., 9-12 & 2-5; Sat.-Sun., 2-5.

The Bastrop Courthouse, the fourth erected on the town square, dates from 1915, with additions. **Bartholomew Methodist Church,** in continuous use from 1825, is located on Hwy. 140 between Bastrop and Bonita. **Rose Theatre,** built in 1927, is a two-story brick, Arts and Crafts-style theatre with cast cement details, in which performances are regularly held. (318-647-3633) **North Louisiana Cotton Festival and Fair** in mid-October features carnival rides and handcrafts. **Morehouse Arts and Crafts Days,** first Saturday in November, is held in the downtown Bastrop business district.

BIENVILLE-ST. DENIS TRAIL: follows La. 2 from Bastrop to Mer Rouge. The two explorers on their map-making expedition gave the name Mer Rouge—Red Sea—to the village because of the red clover that covered the prairie in 1700.

OAK RIDGE: A variety of antebellum homes and historic churches are on tour annually by appointment. (318-244-5435). Excelsior, built in the late 1800s, is filled with antiques and memorabilia. Lovely gardens. On La. 133 in Oak Ridge. Open by appt. Admission. (318-244-6490)

RAYVILLE: Rhymes Memorial Library, built in 1928, is the site of the first public library in the state, in use until 1971. Features changing exhibits of regional history, culture, and arts. Mon.-Thurs., 12-5. (318-728-4127)

OAK GROVE: parish seat of West Carroll Parish, which was created in 1877 when the larger parish of Carroll was subdivided. Old Missouri-Pacific Railroad Depot, on La. 2, was in use as a freight station from 1906 until the 1960s. Fiske Memorial Theatre, Main Street (La. 2) is the site of live performances—schedule available (318-428-3489).

BAYOU MACON (pronounced Mason): divides East and West Carroll. Jesse James and his gang were reputed to have hidden in this vicinity.

POVERTY POINT STATE COMMEMORATIVE AREA: located on La. 577 off La. 134 near Epps. The site of a prehistoric Indian community is the largest complex of ceremonial mounds yet discovered in North America. Tours of the 400-acre park can be taken on foot with trail guide or in motorized tram. Museum with artifacts and interpretive program. Picnic area. Admission. Open Mon.-Sat., 9-5; Sun., 1-5. (318-926-5492) Special programs include Artifact identification weekend, flint knapping seminar, and Native American crafts and dance program. **DELHI:** settled before the Civil War, the nearby swamps offered Jesse James good hiding places. Poverty Point Fall Festival is held in mid-October, featuring craftsmen and entertainment. (318-878-3792)

OLD RIVER AND GASSOWAY LAKES: these two small lakes in the very northeast corner of the state offer fishing, boating, skiing, and swimming.

LAKE PROVIDENCE: the oldest town in Louisiana north of Natchitoches was a trading post during the 1700s and was laid out in 1833. Called Providence, the town was renamed Lake Providence in 1819. Historians surmise that both de Soto and LaSalle may have visited Tensas Indian villages nearby. The scenic oxbow lake is used for fishing and swimming. Only a small portion of **Grant's Canal** remains, seen from Lake or North Hood Streets. The project, commanded by General Grant during the siege of Vicksburg in 1863, was to have connected Lake Providence with the Mississippi River so Union gunboats could bypass Vicksburg, but only one mile was ever completed. Tourism information at East Carroll Chamber of Commerce (318-559-2109). **Soul Food and Heritage Festival**, the second weekend in June, is held on the Courthouse Square and features traditional culture, food, and heritage exhibits and demonstrations. **Port of Lake Providence,** U.S. 65, 2 miles south of Lake Providence, is a still-water harbor, the principal Mississippi River port between Baton Rouge and Helena, Ark. **Sullivan Park**, overlooking the Mississippi River, offers river access and park amenities. **Arlington,** built in 1841, was used during the Civil War as Union Army headquarters. Drive by. **Panola Plantation** offers tours of their pepper sauce production. (318-559-1774) A landmark 15 miles south was named to honor President Theodore Roosevelt, who hunted in the area in 1907 and recorded his adventures in an article, "In the Louisiana Canebrakes."

TALLULAH, founded in 1857, was the site of a U.S.D.A. laboratory in the early 1900s that experimented in insect control for cotton and in the 1920s perfected aerial crop-dusting techniques. **Madison Parish Courthouse,** build by the W.P.A. in the 1930s, encloses the old courthouse, built in 1887. **Talullah Christmas Festival** features lights and downtown displays.

TENSAS RIVER NATIONAL WILDLIFE REFUGE: about 10 miles west of Tallulah, south off U.S. 80, is a 52,000-acre tract incorporating the finest remaining bottomland hardwood in the Mississippi River valley and rare habitat for the black bear. The preserve offers a visitors' center with interpretive program and wildlife exhibits, as well as a boardwalk into the refuge. Fishing on oxbow lakes around the property, some hunting. No camping.(318-574-2664)

MOUND is one of the smallest incorporated towns in the United States. Area information available, Mound Office of Tourism (318-574-5674).

I-20 WESTBOUND LOUISIANA TOURIST INFORMATION CENTER, near the Mississippi border, offers information and brochures, a rest area, and picnic facilities. Open daily, 8:30-5, except Thanksgiving and Christmas. (318-574-5674)

DAVIS ISLAND, located in the Mississippi River between Madison and Tensas parishes. The Bienville-St. Denis map-making expedition landed here in 1700. Jefferson and Joseph E. Davis purchased the land in 1818 and built two plantation homes which were confiscated during the siege of Vicksburg. Neither remains today.

GRANT'S MARCH: The route taken by General Grant's troops during the siege of Vicksburg is marked along La. 605 and 608. All plantations with the exception of Winter Quarters were burned. Winter Quarters, on La. 608 northeast of Newellton, dates to 1800 and was used by General Grant as headquarters during the siege of Vicksburg. Drive-by. **NEWELLTON:** a marble arch inscribed with the Newell family history and an account of the founding of Newellton in 1832 marks the entrance to the Newell family cemetery adjoining the home of founder Edward Drumgould Newell.

LAKE BRUIN STATE PARK, La. 604 between Newellton and St. Joseph, is a small park area beside the 3,000-acre oxbow lake now used for recreation. Fishing, boating, swimming, camping. (318-766-3530)

ST. JOSEPH: The St. Joseph National Register Historic District has been cited as the most intact example of a 19th century Mississippi River levee town north of Natchez, Mississippi. **Tensas Parish Museum,** in the old Snyder House on Plank Road, built circa 1850, is open by appointment. (318-766-3222). The Tensas Parish Library is in the same building, open all year, Mon.-Wed. & Fri., 8-5; Thurs., 8-12; Sat., 9-12. **Tensas Parish Courthouse,** Greek Revival style, was built in 1906 on the site of the original courthouse. Open daily during regular business hours. **Christ Episcopal Church,** on Courthouse Square, is a late-Gothic wooden church built in 1872. Next door, the Bondurant Home (private) is the church rectory. It was the second story of Pleasant View plantation, built in 1852, and moved to the present site in the 1880s. The area is dotted with other significant 19th century structures—in-town residences and plantation homes, some along the River Road—but they are private; occasionally open by appointment. Inquire at the library for local tourist information.

WATERPROOF: Floods and cave-ins forced the town to relocate several times. It finally was moved to higher ground where it was deemed "waterproof." (Its original location is now in Mississippi.) Waterproof First Methodist Church was built in 1871 and moved to its current location in 1881. Area plantation homes dating from early to mid-1800s are private; drive-by only.

TURKEY CREEK GAME AND FISH PRESERVE, on La. 562 west of Wisner. A 3,000-acre property including Turkey Creek Lake. Boating, playgrounds, camping.

WISNER: Catfish processing-plant tours. Located on La. 562, open Mon.-Fri., 9-4. Free.

GILBERT: site of the **Chennault House** (La. 15, south of La. 128) was the boyhood home of World War II hero, Gen. Claire Chennault.

Built in 1910, the Queen Anne Victorian structure is a typical turn-of-the-century cotton planter's home. Currently undergoing restoration—inquire. (318-435-4828)

WINNSBORO: the one-block area surrounding courthouse square has been designated the Jackson Street Historic District. Local tourist information on the parish available at the Franklin Parish Library. (318-435-4336).

BASKIN: Baskin High School is the town's largest, most ornate structure, built in 1925-26. Used as a site for public gatherings. The school's original interior and exterior architectural details are intact.

FORT NECESSITY: located on La. 128 & 562, the original fort was named for George Washington's famous fort. Local legend says the town began when two keelboats—one carrying a cotton gin, the other an iron board mill—ran aground, and after the boatmen failed to free them, they settled there.

BOEUF WILDLIFE MANAGEMENT AREA: a 38,000-acre tract located 10 miles southeast of Columbia on La. 559, offers hunting, fishing, and three camping areas. (318-757-4571)

COLUMBIA: The Caldwell Parish seat hosts the annual Louisiana Art and Folk Festival, featuring arts, crafts, performing arts, and food. Second weekend in October. (318-649-6136). **The Art and Folk Museum,** located on Pearl Street and the Ouachita River, exhibits folk crafts and sponsors programs related to folk culture. (318-649-6722) **United Methodist Church,** built circa 1911, is an interesting Scandinavian Gothic building. Shepis Building, built about 1915 by John Shepis, immigrant Italian architect, is made of handcast concrete "stone" to resemble a villa. **Columbia Heights Cemetery,** one of the most picturesque in the state, contains the graves of early settlers.

LAKE LAFOURCHE: off U.S. 165 between Columbia and Riverton, the 27-mile-long lake offers fishing, hunting, boat launch and rentals, and campsites.

OUACHITA WILDLIFE MANAGEMENT AREA: 12 miles south of Monroe, off La. 841, this 8,700-acre tract offers hunting, trapping by permit, and reservoir fishing. (318-343-4044)

ALTO: The Altus Museum, on La. 15, built in 1917 as a Georgian-style bank, exhibits vintage medical instruments, historic photos and documents, and paintings. (318-248-3508)

RUSSELL SAGE WILDLIFE MANAGEMENT AREA: Over 17,000 acres east of Monroe are dedicated to excellent fishing, bird-watching, hunting, primitive camping. 400 acres 3 miles north of Monroe make up another small area. (318-343-4044)

MONROE/WEST MONROE: Hernando de Soto crossed the

Ouachita River here in 1542; Bienville and St. Denis mapped it in 1700. Though the first white settlers established residence in 1719 and the French trading post was called Prairie des Canots, no permanent community was established until 1763, after the French and Indian War, when Louisiana was ceded to Spain. Don Juan Filhiol completed construction of Fort Miro in 1791. The settlement became known as Monroe in 1819 when its name was changed after the arrival of the first steamboat, the *James Monroe,* named for the fifth president. **The Ouachita River** is considered one of the most scenic and is developed for recreation from the Arkansas border south through Caldwell Parish. It separated Monroe from its livelier counterpart on the west bank, Trenton, now called West Monroe. A bridge was erected in 1882 to connect the two cities.

MONROE/WEST MONROE CONVENTION AND VISITORS BUREAU: 1333 State Farm Drive. Local tourist information, maps, brochures. Open weekdays, 8-5. (318-387-5691). **Northeast Louisiana Arts Council** offers information on special exhibits, performances, and events. (318-396-9520) **MONROE: Old City Cemetery,** 900 DeSiard. Begun in 1825, the cemetery contains tombs, monuments and above-ground crypts unique to the 1800s. Very decorative tombstones. **Old Clerk's Office,** 300 block of St. John. Built in the early 1800s, this small, white stucco building is the oldest public building in Monroe and is constructed of native cypress. Groups by appointment. (318-323-9378). **Monroe National Register Historic District,** centered at 100 S. Grand. These exceptionally well-constructed connecting buildings, built in the late 1800s, overlook the Ouachita River. They cover a city block and are in the process of restoration. **Isaiah Garrett House**, 520 S. Grand, built in 1840, is the only structure remaining in the old frontier style. It was used by Garrett as a law office and is near the site of the original Fort Miro. A museum of Ouachita Parish history, open by appointment. (318-322-6192). **Ouachita Parish Courthouse** was built in 1925, the fourth to stand on the site originally donated by Don Juan Filhiol in 1816. **Masur Museum of Art,** 1400 S. Grand, houses a permanent collection and special exhibits, and offers workshops. Open Tues.-Thurs., 10-6; Fri.-Sun., 2-5. (318-329-2237)

The Emy Lou Biedenharn Foundation, 2004-6 Riverside, runs a three-part attraction, including: Bible Research Museum, a unique, nondenominational Biblical museum housing a large collection of fine antique Bibles, coins, musical instruments, and antique furnishings; Elsong, built in 1914 as the home of Joseph Biedenharn, first bottler of Coca Cola, furnished with the family's collection of elegant furnishings and personal memorabilia; Elsong Gardens, a formal, walled garden, separated into smaller gardens, with musical background in each. The Museum and Elsong are shown by docents. Free. Open Tues.-Fri., 10-4; Sat.-Sun., 2-5 except national holidays. Tours on the hour. (318-387-5281). **Forsythe/Monroe Boat Dock** offers public parking and picnic area on the river. *Twin City Queen,* a 3-decker riverboat, offers sightseeing tours along the Ouachita River on weekends from May-Sept. Departs from Forsythe Dock area. Admission. (318-329-2255). **Forsythe Park,** Riverside at Forsythe, is a city park with the Swayze Natatorium, one of the largest swimming pools in the South (admission), as well as other recreation facilities. The Ouachita River Fest, mid-September weekend, features water entertainment and events on the river and activities in the park. **Louisiana Purchase Gardens and Zoo,** Bernstein Park at Thomas, houses over 800 animals, gardens, and amusement rides. Open daily 10-5. Admission. **Rebecca's Doll Museum,** 4500 Bon Aire, is a collection of over 2000 antique and contemporary dolls. By appt. or chance. Admission. (318-343-3361). Chennault Park and Recreation Complex, named for Gen. Claire Chennault, located on Milhaven Road, features an unusual 18-hole, 225-yard, par 64 frisbee golf course, in addition to tennis courts, archery range, and picnic areas. **Mulberry Grove-Layton Castle,** 1133 S. Grand, a two-story raised cottage built in 1814, was enlarged and changed in 1910 to its present, pink-brick-castle appearance. By appt. only. (318-325-1952 or 387-5691). Admission.

   Gov. Luther E. Hall Home, 1515 Jackson St., is a neo-Georgian mansion built in 1906 by the former governor, now used by the YWCA. Tours by appt. (318-323-1505). **Cooley House,** Grand St., is one of the few remaining homes designed by Walter Burley Giffin, an early associate of Frank Lloyd Wright. Built in 1926, it now houses law offices. Private. **Calhoun Hayride**, open the 1st and 3rd Saturday nights each month in the Calhoun High School Auditorium, features live country, gospel, and bluegrass music. Admission. **Boscobel Cottage,** south of Monroe, was built in 1820 and enlarged in 1840. Restored to show two periods of development. Groups by appt. Admission. (318-325-1550). **Northeast Louisiana University,** 700 University Ave.—Museum of Natural History displays prehistoric Indian artifacts. Open weekdays, 8-4. (318-342-4100). For information on special exhibits and performances on the NLU campus, call 318-342-4198 or 342-2011. **Winterfest,** held on the NLU campus the first three weekends in December, features caroling, fireworks, entertainment, and special Renaissance dinners. Admission to dinners. (318-342-4140). **Krewe of Janus Mardi Gras Parade**—held 2 Saturdays before Mardi

Gras. **Miss Louisiana Pageant** held each June to determine Louisiana's entry to Miss America contest.

CITIES SERVICE WILDLIFE MANAGEMENT AREA, located six miles northeast of Monroe off La. 139 adjacent to Black Bayou Lake. Almost 15,000-acres offer hunting, trapping by permit, and bird-watching. No camping. (318-343-4044)

WEST MONROE: Kiroli Park, off La. 15 north, offers picnic shelters, two miles of paved exercise walkway. **Lazarre Point,** south Riverfront on the Ouachita River, is a sand beach with swimming, boat ramp, picnicking. Fee. **Cheniere Lake Park,** south of West Monroe, is a cypress-studded lake and park offering excellent fishing, nature trail, picnicking, boat ramps, and lodge with kitchen. (318-325-8327). **Bawcomville Recreation Area,** east of La. 34, is a shady park overlooking the Ouachita River with picnic sites and boat ramp. **Old Fashioned Folk Festival,** at the West Monroe Civic Center, held in mid-July, features traditional arts, crafts, and folklife, and entertainment such as barbershop singers, fiddling contest, and square dancing. (318-396-5000). **The Louisiana Passion Play,** recently relocated from Calhoun to a permanent 16,000-seat outdoor amphitheatre carved in a natural hillside setting at the site of Ole Susannah's Country Square, Cheniere Drew Road, north of I-20. The dramatic portrayal of the passion of Jesus of Nazareth unfolds Friday, in May and September, at 8:30 P.M., Thurs.-Sat. during June, July and August, 8:30. Admission. Reservations encouraged. (318-644-2247)

D'ARBONNE NATIONAL WILDLIFE REFUGE, north of West Monroe off La. 143, is a protected habitat for threatened and endangered birds and the American alligator. Bayou D'Arbonne bisects this scenic area.

BIENVILLE-ST. DENIS HISTORIC TRAIL roughly approximates La. 34 in Jackson Parish near Chatham.

JACKSON-BIENVILLE WILDLIFE MANAGEMENT AREA, located in both Jackson and Bienville parishes, is 31,000-acres accessible from U.S. 167 and La. 147. (For Ruston information, see Shreveport area.) Fishing, hunting, bird-watching, and camping available. (318-377-3575)

QUITMAN/BEECH SPRINGS: The Jimmy Davis Tabernacle, located on the Beech Springs Road, is the homeplace of the former governor and his family. Gospel singing meets are held here, as is the annual "homecoming" and tour, first Sunday in October. (318-259-7516)

CHATHAM: Brooklyn Church and Cemetery, on La. 44 south of town, was built in 1902 and is a rare example of an almost unchanged turn-of-the-century frame church.

JONESBORO: the parish seat for Jackson Parish was once connected to Hodge by the world's longest wooden sidewalk. The Jackson Parish Junior Livestock Show is held in late September.

POVERTY POINT

At certain times, the park manager says he can feel the presence of the Ancient Ones. Not like ghosts that haunt a house, but as the spirit of the place, in that peculiar sense of another dimension. The Ancient Ones are forever a part of this site.

Of course it sounds absurd, irrational. But no one questions the mystical quality of Stonehenge, that arrangement of giant boulders on the green plains of central England. So why should the evocation of ancient peoples in a quiet corner of what is now northeast Louisiana seem odd? Is it more difficult to believe that five or six thousand people lived here three milennia ago, on this land along Bayou Macon, about the same time the Egyptian pyramids were being erected for desert pharaohs? Is it rational to accept the scientists' explanation that they were a large, sophisticated civilization who cooked their food in earthen convection ovens, hunted with a trove of advanced weapons, worked with a cache of well-crafted tools, and traded and travelled with other cultures as far away as present-day Appalachia and Michigan?

Did these prehistoric people really model aesthetically appealing effigies of clay, create attractive beaded jewelry, live in huts along long, concentric, manmade ridges to escape the always-present threat of flooding, and pray at an enormous earth mound shaped like a bird in flight that they constructed from infinite basketsful of earth dug with sticks?

These are the facts about Poverty Point, the beliefs of archeologists based on digs and analyses of what they have found at this site called one of the most significant on the North American continent. Through careful inquiry and systematic study of the tangible evidence—artifacts, "cultural garbage," mounds, and rings, they have pieced together an astounding picture of an extraordinary civilization. Yes, the archeologists assert, these ancient ones lived here and did all these things and more.

For most people, the discovery of a Civil War minie ball is a source of great excitement, a special bond with history; finding a relic from

Bienville's exploration would be beyond comprehension. So the extraordinary uncovering of pottery shards, arrowheads, clay cooking balls, and thousands of other artifacts that pre-date the Greek and Roman Empires seems utterly fantastic in the pastoral setting of northeast Louisiana.

The Poverty Point Commemorative Area Visitors Center presents this story, via an introductory slide show, in a well explicated museum exhibit displaying many of the fascinating artifacts, as well as by a guided walk along the well-marked trail. And archeological study continues; there is so much more to learn, to understand, to document about this ancient culture.

So is it really so remarkable that, when the wind rustles in the trees and a nameless stillness fills the site, the presence of the Ancient Ones doesn't seem quite so farfetched after all?

Ancient Indian burial mounds, Poverty Point. (Photograph by Mary Ann Sternberg)

2

Shreveport and the Northwest

The Red River stretches through this section of the state, but, until 1833, when Captain Henry Shreve was commissioned by the federal government to remove a 165-mile-long log entanglement, this great river wasn't navigable. This area includes the second oldest settlement in Louisiana—Natchitoches—as well as considerable Spanish/Texas influence, dating from the period when the Sabine River was established as the boundary between the French and Spanish territories with a 50-mile strip of neutral, "no-man's land" on either side of it. Northwest Louisiana's topography ranges from the most dramatic hill areas in Louisiana, including the state's highest "mountain," to almost flatland. Ten parishes comprise this section of the state—Caddo, Bossier, Webster, Claiborne, Lincoln, Bienville, Red River, Natchitoches, De Soto, and Sabine. Shreveport is its largest city.

THREE STATES MARKER: At La. 1 and Tx. 77 is the meeting point of the boundary lines of Louisiana, Texas, and Arkansas.

RODESSA: Rodessa itself was a thriving town that popped up almost overnight with the discovery of the famous Rodessa Oil Field in 1935. Off La. 168 west of Rodessa are two brick columns marking the site of **Frog Level,** a now-defunct 19th century community. **The Northwest Louisiana Wild Flower Trail** passes through Rodessa, east on La. 168 to U.S. 71 south. Late April-early May.

VIVIAN: The Chamber of Commerce, W. Front at Louisiana, in the old depot, offers tourist information (318-375-5300) and houses the Redbud Museum which contains artwork and historic memorabilia of northwest Louisiana. Open Mon.-Sat., 1-5. **The Redbud Festival** centers on hundreds of blooming redbud trees. Arts and crafts, music, parade, and pageant. Third Saturday in March. **Country Junction**

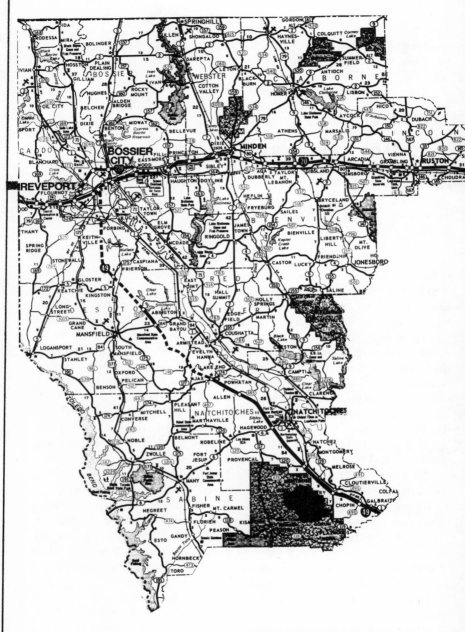

Shreveport Area

building, a turn-of-the-century building constructed of 175,000 molded, handmade bricks from local red clay.

OIL CITY: the site of the first oil well drilled in northwest Louisiana in 1906. **The Caddo-Pine Island Museum,** located in 3 early-1900s boomtown buildings, houses exhibits of north Caddo history and the oil industry. Open Mon.-Fri., 9-5. Admission (318-995-6845). **Discovery Well** is an exact replica of the first oil well built in the area. **Caddo Lake,** crossing the Louisiana-Texas border, is a large recreational lake with boating, skiing, fishing, hunting, and camping. **Earl Williamson Park,** on the banks of Caddo Lake, offers boat ramp, fishing pier, picnicking, recreation, and campsites. Fee. **Gusher Days Festival,** celebrating the oil industry, offers music, arts and crafts, games, contests, and a parade. First weekend in May.

MOORINGSPORT: on the shore of Caddo Lake, Caddo Indians established their villages. In the early 20th century, the area supported a thriving pearl industry.

SODA LAKE WILDLIFE MANAGEMENT AREA: a 1,200-acre tract for hunting and permit-trapping. No camping. Off Blanchard-Dixie Road. (318-377-3575)

BLANCHARD: The Walter B. Jacobs Park, a 160-acre preserve, features an interpretive center with hands-on exhibits and 5 miles of well-marked nature trails through hardwood bottomlands and abundant flora and fauna. Open Wed.-Sat., 9-5; Sun., 1-5. (318-929-2806). **Poke Salad Festival** honors the edible wild green that helped Depression-era folks survive. Parades, contests, entertainment and Miss Louisiana preliminary pageant. Second weekend in May.

CROSS LAKE: this reservoir source of Shreveport's drinking water was formed in 1926 and offers recreation such as fishing and boating. Along South Lakeshore Drive is Ford Park, especially for children, with woods, old army tank, steam locomotive, and electric trolley. Open daily, 8-sunset.

SHREVEPORT: Shreveport was a frontier town settled by Carolinians until 1833 when Captain Henry Shreve was commissioned to unclog the Red River logjam. The Caddo Indians in 1835 sold their land claims, which were indirectly bought by Shreve. When the logjam cleared in 1836, Shreve's acreage in the Shreve Town Company soon became part of the town. Shreveport was recognized by the state legislature as a town in 1839 and grew into the major commercial center of Northwest Louisiana, serving as the state's capital from 1863-65.

Shreveport/Bossier Convention and Tourist Bureau, 629 Spring Street, offers tourist information, brochures, and maps. Open 8:30-5, weekdays. (318-222-93911 or 800-551-8682). For information on special performances, events, or exhibits, contact the Shreveport Regional Arts Council (318-673-7727).

Louisiana State Exhibit Museum, 3015 Greenwood Road, an Art Deco structure opened in 1939, features museum, gallery, and auditorium. Under the marble rotunda are murals, paintings, historic artifacts including a prehistoric canoe, and dioramas of Louisiana history. Open Tues.-Sat., 9-4:30; Sun., 1-5. (318-632-2020) **Louisiana State Fairgrounds,** between I-20 and U.S. 80, hosts the Louisiana State Fair, one of the top 10 fairs in the nation. Entertainment, livestock competition, horse shows, rodeo, midway, and exhibits. Last ten days in October. Admission. The SPAR Planetarium offers special sky shows and laser lights. (318-673-7827). **Independence Bowl,** the first NCAA-sanctioned post-season college football game, held at Independence Stadium on the fairgrounds in mid-December. Other related entertainment. Admission. (318-221-0712). **Shreveport Captains,** a farm team for the San Francisco Giants, play the only professional baseball in the state. Fair Grounds Filed. Admission. (318-636-5555). **Coates Bluff Postique,** 2400 Texas. In the lobby of the U.S. Post Office is a replica of an historic post office constructed and furnished with vintage materials to show early postal operations. Open weekdays, 8:30-4. (318-677-2240) **Holy Cross Church,** Texas at Cotton, is a neo-Gothic structure dedicated in 1905. The oldest continuously in-use church in Shreveport incorporates the altar, pews, French glass windows, and chancel rail from the original church in the chapel. The original cornerstone, from 1850, is imbedded in the chapel wall.

Strand Theatre, Crockett at Louisiana, built in 1925, is a restored neo-baroque theatre, one of the few ornate theatres extant. It is listed on the National Register and contains an impressive, functional pipe organ. Open for performances or by appt. (318-226-8555). **Holy Trinity Catholic Church,** Marshall at Fannin, was built in 1896 in the Romanesque style. It is the oldest standing church in Shreveport and has stained glass windows memorializing five Catholic priests who died during the yellow fever epidemic in 1873. **Caddo Parish Courthouse,** 500 Texas, was built of limestone in 1926 and is considered a fine example of American monumental architecture. An original courthouse stood on the site as early as 1860. The Confederate Monument, unveiled in 1906, signifies the site of the last Confederate flag lowered after the end of the Civil War. **The Shreve Memorial Library,** built in 1912 in Italian Renaissance style, originally served as the U.S. Post Office from its construction until 1974. The library contains a notable genealogy collection, a rare book collection, and a petroleum and geology room, in addition to general collections. **Spring Street Museum,**

515 Spring, was built in 1866 as a bank. It now houses a collection of Victorian furnishings and rotating exhibits of historic memorabilia of the region. Open by appt. Admission. (318-424-0964) **Shreve Square** is a restored city block of warehouse spaces from the Victorian era. **Barnwell Art and Garden Center,** 501 Fant Pkwy., is dedicated to art and horticulture, featuring a domed conservatory with a collection of assorted flora, a fragrance garden for the visually impaired, outdoor gardens overlooking the Red River, and changing exhibits of flora-related art. Open Mon.-Fri., 9-4:30; weekends, 1-5. (318-673-7703). **Clyde Fant Parkway,** a 4 1/2-mile green strip along the Red River with walking/biking/jogging path, frisbee golf course, picnic facilities, and playgrounds. **Sports Museum of Champions**, 600 Clyde Fant Parkway, features artifacts and memorabilia of famous sports figures from Shreveport. Tues-Sun, 1-5. Admission. (318-227-0238) **Downtown historic tour** follows a brochure published by the Shreveport/Bossier Convention & Tourist Bureau through the downtown area. **Austin Place**, especially the restored 700 block, reflects a late 19th century residential neighborhood restored to its original grandeur. **Fort Humbug Historical Marker,** on the grounds of the Veterans Hospital, marks the fort used to guard the city from Union gunboats. Charred logs were placed along the river to fool the scouts into believing that the fort was well protected, thus the name. **Symphony House,** Woodlawn, was built in 1872 by Col. Robert Lindsay in a transition style between Greek Revival and late Victorian. Listed on the National Register, open weekdays, 9-5. **Centenary College** is the oldest liberal arts college west of the Mississippi River. **The Meadows Museum,** on the Centenary campus, at 2911 Centenary Drive, contains the extraordinary collection of oils, watercolors, and drawings by French artist Jean Despujols expressing visual reality of the Indo-Chinese culture and landscape, as well as travelling exhibits. Open Tues.-Fri., 1-5; weekends, 2-5. (318-869-5169). For special exhibits, performances, and events on the Centenary Campus, inquire. (318-869-5703). **Clyde Connell Contemporary Art Center**, 614 Edwards Ave., serves as a gallery and arts and crafts educational facility. **R.W. Norton Art Gallery,** 4747 Creswell, situated in a wooded, 40-acre landscape, houses a collection of American and European art spanning 300 years in one of the largest private galleries in the state. It is noted for its extensive holdings of western art. Special exhibits are also shown. Open Tues.-Sun., 1-5. (318-865-4201). **Highland-Fairfield Home** tour follows a map available from the Shreveport Bossier Tourist and Convention Bureau that winds through Shreveport's elegant old residential area. Most homes are private; a few are open by appt. A special Spring Tour

is held annually in mid-April, with several residences open and refreshments served. Admission. (318-222-9391)

Bickham Dickson Park, located in a natural wooded setting with trails and a 200-acre oxbow lake, offers hayrides, biking, fishing. (318-798-1841). **Pioneer Heritage Folk Center,** La. 1 at Louisiana State University-Shreveport, located in the Caspiana House which was built in 1856, moved to this site in 1977. The exhibit of several types of authentic pioneer-era buildings of north Louisiana enables visitors to see how early settlers lived. Interpretive program and culture lab. Open Sundays, 1:30-4:30. Admission. (318-797-5332). **Hamel's Amusement Park,** E. 70th, offers north Louisiana's largest roller coaster and other rides. Admission. **Red River Revel,** a 9-day festival in October held along the Red River in downtown Shreveport, offers arts and crafts, juried art show, performance entertainment, and food, with associated programs and demonstrations. (318-424-4000). **Holiday in Dixie,** a 10-day festivity in April, features a parade, entertainment, treasure hunt, games, contests, and races. (318-865-5555)

BOSSIER CITY: originally called Bennett's Bluff, the community was renamed Bossier City in the early 20th century after General Pierre Evariste John Baptist Bossier, a famous Creole general who helped settle the area. It is located just across the Red River from Shreveport. For information on special exhibits, performances and events, contact the Bossier Arts Council. (318-741-8310). **Louisiana Downs,** 8000 U.S. 80 east, is a top-quality thoroughbred race track with pari-mutuel betting. Season is May-November. No minors. Admission. (800-551-RACE). **Shed Road,** a nine-mile, covered log turnpike built in the 1870s to facilitate the transportation of cotton and supplies. Historic marker at Airline and Shed Rd. **Mike Wood Memorial Park,** Shady Grove at Dennis, includes a fitness trail, Olympic-size swimming pool, tennis courts, and picnic facilities. **Barksdale Air Force Base,** access from U.S. 71, is the headquarters of the U.S. Eighth Air Force and one of the most significant airports in the world. It is the home of the Strategic Air Command. The Eighth Air Force Museum, located near the north gate, houses an impressive display of aircraft and exhibits of U.S. aviation history. During the Holiday in Dixie, Barksdale hosts an open house and air show. Bus tours of the base are available by appt. with 3 weeks notice. For museum or tour information, call Barksdale Public Affairs Office (318-456-3065). **Touchstone Museum of Natural History,** U.S. 80, houses dioramas of wildlife in their natural habitat. Tues-Sat, 9-5; Sun, 1-5. (318-949-2323)

GREENWOOD: The American Rose Center and **American Rose Society Garden,** Jefferson-Paige Road, is the headquarters of America's largest plant society and the largest rose garden in the country. Open daily mid-April through October. Admission. **Christmas in Roseland** is a festival of Christmas lights in the Rose Gardens from the day after Thanksgiving to New Year's Eve from dusk to 10 PM. Entertainment. (318-938-5402). **Boothill Speedway,** Cemetery Road, a quarter-mile, banked drag racing track, hosts races each weekend, March-November. **Pioneer Days,** the last weekend in September, includes arts and crafts, pioneer dress, contests, races, and a barbecue.

1-20 EASTBOUND LOUISIANA TOURIST INFORMATION CENTER, near the Texas border, offers picnic facilities and rest area, tourist information, maps, and brochures. Open daily, 8:30-5. Closed Thanksgiving and Christmas. (318-938-5613)

CYPRESS-BLACK BAYOU RECREATION AREA: Linton Rd., between Bossier City and Benton, consists of two man-made lakes containing 3,700-acres. Recreation, camping, swimming, fishing, nature trails. Bossier Parish Nature Study Center contains collections of native plants and animals. Interpretive center open by appt. Facilities for the handicapped. Admission. (318-965-0007).

ROCKY MOUNT: a Civil War village where the Hughes Home, a log dogtrot house, is known as the seat of Secession because of the meeting of Bossier Parish citizens who voted to secede from the Union in 1860, before the formal outbreak of the Civil War. **Rocky Mount historical trail** is a 10-mile hiking trail past an Indian village site, Coushatta Bluff, and plantation houses. Unmarked—request information.

PLAIN DEALING: host of a Dogwood Festival featuring a beautiful, 14-mile dogwood trail. Late March-early April.

BODCAU WILDLIFE MANAGEMENT AREA: over 32,000-acres of pine and hardwood forest features camping, fishing, bird-watching, and hunting. (318-377-3575)

SPRINGHILL: site of the Lumberjack Festival, with arts and crafts, antique and classic car show, games and contests, and entertainment. Second weekend in October.

MINDEN: the parish seat of Webster Parish was settled about 1837 and named for the birthplace of its founder's parents in Germany. Dorcheat Bayou is a natural scenic waterway today offering excellent fishing and hunting. It once served as the chief means of transportation for the area. **Webster Parish Library** is a fine example of Spanish Colonial Revival architecture. **First Baptist Church,** established in 1844, boasts the grandfather of the former First Lady, Lady Bird Johnson, as its founder and first pastor. **Bayou Raceway** features auto races.

GERMANTOWN: on Webster Parish Road 114. Founded in 1835 by German emigres seeking individual rights and freedom from persecution, this town operated for 37 years as a communal system. Only a few buildings remain and are called the Germantown Museum. Exhibits include artifacts of the settlement, documents, letters, tools, and furniture. Open Wed.-Sat., 10-5, Sun., 1-5. Admission. (318-377-1875)

KISATCHIE NATIONAL FOREST, CANEY LAKE RECREATION AREA: off La. 159, offers bird-watching, camping, hunting, swimming, boating, skiing, campsites, nature trails, and boat ramps. Admission.

HAYNESVILLE: site of the Claiborne Parish Fair and the Northwest Louisiana Dairy Festival during the last week of September.

HOMER: the names of Homer and its neighbors, Arcadia, Athens, and Sparta, were inspired by an interest in contemporary excavations in Greece, reflected in the local architecture. **Claiborne Parish Courthouse,** W. Main, was built in Greek Revival style in 1860 and is still in use. Confederate soldiers gathered here before departing for the Civil War. Open Mon.-Fri., 9-4. **Ford Museum,** 519 S. Main, exhibits artifacts and memorabilia of pioneer north Louisiana hill country. Fri and Sun, 2-4; Sat, 10-2. Admission. (318-927-9190) (318-927-9190). Both are part of the Homer Historic District. **Claiborne Jubilee,** held at Courthouse Square, features sidewalk art shows, parades, costumes and contests. End of April or early May. (318-927-3271). **Claiborne Parish Christmas Festival,** held the second weekend in December, features a parade and activities on the courthouse square. **Claiborne Parish Tourist Information: (318-927-3271 or 927-2223).**

LAKE CLAIBORNE STATE PARK: on La. 146, about 7 miles southeast of Homer, is a 620-acre facility offering fishing, swimming, camping, picnicking, boat launches, and rentals. 6400 acre Lake Claiborne is one of the deepest lakes in north Louisiana. (318-927-2976)

WHITE LIGHTNING ROAD: La. 146 was heavily travelled by bootleggers during prohibition, with many stills located off this road.

ARIZONA COMMUNITY: off La. 2 on Hwy. 86, the site of the earliest textile mill in the parish is commemorated by the Arizona Museum, housing local history and artifacts. By appt. (318-927-3614). A church, established in 1866, and a cemetery with a grave of the daughter of a Revolutionary War soldier and several unknown Confederates are also here.

SUMMERFIELD: Alberry Wasson Homeplace, between Homer and Junction City on La. 2, is the only two-story double-dogtrot loghouse in Louisiana. Built about 1850, it is on the National Register and interprets pioneer life and history of the area. Sun. 2-5 or by appt. (318-927-2754)

KISATCHIE NATIONAL FOREST, CANEY DISTRICT: on Parish Rd. 237 off La. 9, Caney Lake offers fishing, boating, camping, picnicking, bird-watching, and swimming. (318-927-2061)

CLAIBORNE TEMPLE INDIAN MOUNDS: off La. 9, these five historic mounds date from 300-800 A.D.

JUNCTION CITY: part in Arkansas, part in Louisiana, with a marker on the town's main street distinguishing the state line.

LISBON: the **Rocky Springs Baptist Church,** built before 1845 and site of the 1886 Louisiana Baptist Convention.

GILL'S FERRY: the only public access in Lincoln Parish to Lake D'Arbonne. Boat launch, picnicking. Off La. 151 to Parish Rd. 5501.

DUBACH: "Dogtrot Capital of Louisiana." The **Autrey House,** built circa 1846, is a handhewn log dogtrot house restored to its original appearance. Family cemetery adjoins. On La. 152. **Dubach House,** built 1901, was the home of Fred B. Dubach, founder of the Dubach Lumber Co., for whom the town was named. On the National Register. By appt. (318-777-3335) Dubach Chicken Festival is held the fourth weekend in September. (318-777-3321)

VIENNA (pronounced vi-anna): this is the oldest Louisiana town west of the Ouachita River and north of Natchitoches and was an overnight stop between Monroe and Shreveport on the stage coach line, but the advent of the railroad five miles south moved the parish seat of government to Ruston. The 140-year-old cemetery and the antebellum Vienna Baptist Church are open to the public. **The Vienna Post Office** was established in 1838.

THE OLD WIRE ROAD: named after the telegraph line strung in 1857 from Lake Providence to Shreveport, this route was cut through the forests of north Louisiana for covered wagons going west and later became the stage coach line. Historical marker on U.S. 167 at Vienna, on La. 146 and La. 3072.

LINCOLN PARISH PARK, located off La. 33 north of Ruston, is a 260-acre landscaped park with walking tails, boat rentals, and a beach. Admission. (318-251-5156)

RUSTON: Ruston, named for Robert E. Russ, who contracted with the Vicksburg, Shreveport and Pacific Railroad to locate a line in 1884. The railroad was supposedly nicknamed the VS&P—Very Slow and Pokey—by passengers. **Ruston-Lincoln Parish Visitors Bureau** offers information, maps, and brochures. 609 N. Vienna. (318-255-2031). The same building, the Kidd-Davis Home, built in 1886, houses the Lincoln Parish Museum. Open Tues.-Fri., 8:30-4:30. **Old Dixie**

Theatre, 206 N. Vienna, was built in 1920 and features a spectacular chandelier. Regular Saturday night live entertainment. Admission. (318-255-6081). Scattered homes and buildings are listed on the National Register. **Railroad Park,** Park Ave., offers a rose garden, outdoor amphitheatre, and fountains. **Piney Hills Gallery,** 206 Park Ave., is a nonprofit gallery featuring original work by regional artists and craftsmen. Tues-Sat, 10-4. (318-255-7234) **Louisiana Tech University** began as Ruston College, then became the Industrial Institute and College of Louisiana in 1894. Inquire about special exhibits and performances on campus (318-257-3060). Wiley Tower is a campus landmark housing the university's art gallery, which features changing exhibits. The Planetarium, with Spitz A-4 projector, is open to the public by appt. The Louisiana Tech Arboretum, south of U.S. 80 and east of Tech Farm Road, is a 50-acre site with recreation area and a variety of representative species from the United States and other countries. LA Tech Conservatory, Lomax Hall, has a display of tropical plants. **The Dairy Farm and Processing Plant** and other campus facilities may be of interest. **Garden of Prayer,** near Cedarton, on Paris Rd. 506, located behind the Rock Corner Baptist Church, is a small garden open to the public. **Louisiana Peach Festival,** held the second and third week in June, celebrates Lincoln Parish's famous peaches. (Ask for information about the location of orchards.) Parades, arts and crafts, dance, cooking contest, entertainment. **Louisiana Passion Play, in Calhoun, east of Ruston on Parish Rd. 442, depicting the life, crucifixion, resurrection and ascension of Jesus Christ, staged in an outdoor amphitheatre. Fri and Sat., July and August, at 8:30 PM. Reservations; admission. (318-644-2247)**

GRAMBLING: site of Grambling State University, which has produced a record number of professional sports players and has one of the most famous marching bands in the country. Inquire about Lyceum Series lecture and performances and special exhibits. (318-247-3811)

SIMSBORO: an historical marker designates where James Monroe Sims founded the town in 1848. **Daniels House** is a pre-Civil War log dogtrot located off La. 147 southwest of Simsboro. **Walnut Creek Baptist Church** was built in 1870 but the cemetery dates from 1846. On the National Register. North of Simsboro on Paris Rd. 3.

MOUNT LEBANON: founded in 1836 by Carolina settlers, the town is considered one of the best examples of Anglo-Saxon settlement in Louisiana, designed in the then-popular parallelogram shape. During the Civil War, the town was one of three communities in Louisiana chosen to design and issue a Confederate stamp; the resulting reversed printing makes these stamps collectors items today. **Mt. Lebanon Baptist Church,** organized in 1837, was host to the organization of the Louisiana Baptist Convention in 1848. The present structure, dating from 1857, retains the original furnishings, including divided pews and hand-planed pulpit. On the National Register. **The Down Home, Colbert Place, Stage Coach Inn, Thurmond Place, the Dog Trot, Wayside Cottage,** and the **Smith Home** were built in the mid-19th century and are on the National Register. **The Stagecoach Museum,** featuring local historical memorabilia and artifacts from Mount Lebanon's heyday as a stagecoach stop, is open Fri.-Sun., 2-5. **The Stagecoach Trail Tour** of homes is held the first Sunday in May.

AMBROSE MOUNTAIN: La. 154 south of Mt. Lebanon is the site of a marker designating where Bonnie Parker and Clyde Barrow were killed by law enforcement officers in 1934.

DRISKILL MOUNTAIN: north of Hwy. 507 above Bienville, this is the highest point in Louisiana, with an elevation of 535 feet.

JACKSON-BIENVILLE WILDLIFE MANAGEMENT AREA: a 31,000-acre tract of pine and hardwoods forest, accessible from La. 147 and La. 155, offers hunting and trapping by permit. (See Northeast Louisiana)

KEPLER LAKE: off La. 507 is a deep, scenic body for fishing, boating, and outdoor recreation.

LAKE BISTINEAU STATE PARK: near Doyline, east of La. 163. The lake was created by damming Loggy Bayou. Picnicking, swimming beach, boat launch and rentals, cabins, and camping. Admission. (318-745-3503)

LOGGY BAYOU WILDLIFE MANAGEMENT AREA: off U.S. 71, the 3,600-acre tract offers hunting, primitive camping, nature trail, and boat ramp. (318-377-3575)

MILL CREEK RESERVOIR: this manmade reservoir north of Saline on La. 155 offers excellent fishing and boating.

READHIMER: off La. 9, between Saline and Campti, in a 120-acre pine forest, is **Briarwood,** the preserve and wild gardens of Louisiana naturalist Caroline Dorman, who specialized in Louisiana and southern native plants. Open March-May, August and November, Sat., 9-5; Sun., 12-5. Admission. (318-576-3523.)

BLACK AND CLEAR LAKES: off La. 9, are excellent for fishing. The Northwest Louisiana Game and Fish Preserve, between La. 9 and 408, offers picnicking, hiking, and camping.

COUSHATTA: named for the Indian tribe who inhabited the area. **The Red River Parish Courthouse,** called "Hanging Tower," is a classic style building dating from 1926 when the original courthouse burned. Inquire at Courthouse for parish tourist information. **The Calaboose,** or old jail, is located behind the fire station. An historical marker designates the site of a riot during Reconstruction. **The Coushatta Depot,** the restored railroad station, serves as a quilting center. **Front Street** is an area of restored buildings. **The Coushatta Lignite Festival** celebrates the local industry in April. The **Red River Bluegrass Festival** celebrates bluegrass music during the summer.

ARMISTEAD: site of the Armistead Cotton Gin Company, offering tours during ginning season by appt. (318-932-3403)

WALLACE LAKE: south of Shreveport, offers fishing and boating.

STONEWALL: founded during Reconstruction and named for Gen. "Stonewall" Jackson. **All Saints Episcopal Chapel,** originally part of Allendale Plantation, is one of two remaining plantation chapels in the state. It has handmade rails and altar, stained glass windows, and a family cemetery. By appt. (318-925-9885).

KEATCHIE: on La. 5 (pronounced "kee-chi," from an Indian word meaning "panther"), is a small, antebellum community and the site of one of the oldest Masonic Lodges in the south. **Keatchie Presbyterian Church,** built in 1856, served as a treatment center for wounded Confederate troops from the Battle of Mansfield. **Keatchie Methodist Church** was also built in the 1850s. **Confederate Memorial Cemetery,** La. 172 west of town, contains the graves of 76 Confederate soldiers and a "grave house," derived from an Indian custom for protecting the body of the deceased. **Keatchie Heritage Days,** held each October, features folklife exhibits of quilting, soap-making, pottery-making, and entertainment.

LOGANSPORT: three acre site 4 miles northwest of town on La. 764 marks the Dry Line Boundary, the 1841 boundary between the United States and the Republic of Texas. **River City Fest,** held the first weekend in May on the banks of the Sabine River, offers arts and crafts, food, and beauty pageant.

TOLEDO BEND RESERVOIR: a 182,000-acre manmade lake was formed by damming the Sabine River. Oak Ridge park features camping and cabins, and hiking. Boating, fishing, and hunting available along the length of the reservoir.

MANSFIELD: this now quiet and charming Southern town was the site of very heavy fighting during the Civil War. Confederate generals Dick Taylor and Alexander Mouton planned the Battle of Mansfield under a large oak tree on Polk Street. **DeSoto Parish Tourist Bureau** offers information, brochures, and maps. Courthouse. (318-872-1177). **The DeSoto Arts Council** offers information on special exhibits, performances, and events. (318-872-5710). **Mansfield Episcopal**

Church contains a memorial to the Confederate troops killed at the battle. **Rock Chapel**, La. 509 east of Mansfield, is a small, Gothic-style chapel built in 1891 by the Carmelite Monks. **Louisiana Blueberry Festival** is held the third week in June and features parades, dancing, food, and crafts on the Courthouse Square.

MANSFIELD STATE COMMEMORATIVE AREA: 4 miles south of Mansfield on La. 175 is the site of a significant Civil War battle on April 8, 1864. Gen. Nathaniel Banks, with an army of 36,000 Union troops, was defeated by Confederate generals E. Kirby-Smith and Dick Taylor leading less than 9,000 men. It was the last great Confederate victory and the last major Louisiana battle. The 44-acre park includes markers describing battle action, interpretive program, and museum with maps, pictures, and artifacts. Open daily, 9 to 5. Admission. (318-872-1474)

PLEASANT HILL: Union troops retreated to Pleasant Hill after the Battle of Mansfield. A reenactment of the Battle of Pleasant Hill, 3 miles north of town, takes place on the weekend nearest the battle date, April 9. Along La. 175 are 7 historical markers designating important points along their route.

REBEL STATE COMMEMORATIVE AREA: 3 miles north of Marthaville on La. 1221, this 31-acre site contains the grave of an unknown Confederate who was separated from his unit and killed here. The park has a stage and amphitheatre and is dedicated to country and bluegrass music. Interpretive program. Summer concerts and a fiddling championship in October are held. (318-472-6255)

LOS ADAES STATE COMMEMORATIVE AREA: on La. 6 east of Robeline is the site of the Spanish fort founded in 1721 that served as the capital of the Spanish Province of Texas for 53 years. The original fort, so placed to defend against the French settlers, included a population of about 300, a mission, and 40 houses, as determined by archeological excavation. Programming in progress. (318-472-9449)

FORT JESUP STATE COMMEMORATIVE AREA: located on La. 6, formerly the Camino Real, the old Spanish Cavalry route to Mexico City, was established in 1822 by General Zachary Taylor to protect settlers from outlaws who hid in the "neutral strip" between the United States and Texas. In 1837, under Zachary Taylor, it was the largest fort in the United States. The 21-acre site contains the original kitchen and a reconstructed officers building which serves as a museum with interpretive program. Open Mon.-Sat., 9-5; Sun., 1-5. (318-256-4117)

ZWOLLE: pronounced "zwah-lee," a town with a Spanish heritage dating back to the Spanish mission and military post at Los Adaes in 1717 but with a Dutch name, because a Dutch stockholder of the

Kansas City Southern Railroad named it. Headquarters of the Southeast Outdoor Press Association, the largest regional association of outdoor writers in the country, the town hosts an annual Tamale Fiesta the second weekend in October, to commemorate its Spanish history. Parade, music, arts and crafts, tamales and other food, entertainment. Also metallic silhouette shooting competition. (318-645-9594)

NORTH TOLEDO BEND STATE PARK: located 9 miles southwest of Zwolle off La. 3229. 900-acre site on a peninsula in Toledo Bend Reservoir. Visitor Center, swimming pool, picnicking, camping, cabins, boat launch, fishing, and hiking. Admission. (318-645-4715)

SABINE WILDLIFE MANAGEMENT AREA: west of La. 171, the 12,500-acre tract of pine and hardwood offers hunting, trapping by permit, and bird-watching. No camping. (318-487-5885)

LOUISIANA TOURIST INFORMATION CENTER: La. 6, west of Many on Toledo Bend Reservoir, offers tourist information, maps, brochures. Open daily 8-4:30; closed Thanksgiving and Christmas. (318-256-5185)

MERRITT MOUNTAIN PARK AND TOM SAWYER BOAT CHAPEL: located on La. 6, east of bridge on Toledo Bend, the nondenominational church park offers picnicking, swimming, hiking, and the boat chapel, a replica of a Mississippi River paddlewheeler used for group activities, with a whistle from one of the old paddlewheelers.

MANY: pronounced "man-ee," was founded by Belgians in 1843 as a trading post for Fort Jesup. **Sabine Parish Tourist and Recreation Commission** offers information, maps, and brochures for Sabine Parish. 920 Fisher Road. (318-256-5880). **Fort Jesup State Commemorative Area,** 6 miles east of Many on La. 6, includes original kitchen and mess hall and museum of officers' quarters of 1822 U.S. Army border fort. Open daily, 9-5, except holidays. Admission. 318-256-4117). Part of the **Camino Real** crosses the city as San Antonio Avenue. **St. John the Baptist Catholic Church,** on La. 6, was built in Spanish missionary style and reflects the area's 83 years under Spanish rule. **A Christmas Parade** is held downtown the second Saturday in December.

FISHER: located east of La. 171, this small, somewhat-intact community was founded in 1897 as a sawmill company town. **Sawmill Days,** held the fourth weekend in May, celebrates the town's history with rides, logging contests, reunion, food, and entertainment. (318-256-2913)

FLORIEN: site of the Sabine Freestate Festival on the second weekend in November, celebrating the pioneer spirit derived from this area's no-man's-land designation between the United States and Texas.

Treasure hunt, syrup mill, arts and crafts, entertainment. (318-256-5880)

HODGES GARDENS: on U.S. 171 south of Florien. A 4,700-acre, private, carefully planned "garden in the forest" containing natural woodlands with wildlife, landscaped gardens, pools, waterfalls, and a lake. Panoramic observation points, picnic facilities, greenhouses, and conservatory. Open 8-5 daily except holidays. Admission. (318-586-3523). **Easter Sunrise Services. Christmas Festival,** lights in the gardens.

KISATCHIE NATIONAL FOREST, KISATCHIE DISTRICT: Kisatchie is an Indian word meaning "long cane." This district off La. 117 contains 98,000-acres and is unusual in Louisiana for its rock outcroppings and valleys and mesas. Longleaf Vista Recreation Area has nature trails, bird-watching, picnicking, hiking, and driving trails. The Long Leaf Trail leads through the Red Dirt Game Preserve, where backpacking and primitive camping are popular. (318-352-2568)

CHOPIN: site of **Little Eva Plantation,** named for the plantation in *Uncle Tom's Cabin,* is the largest and one of the oldest pecan plantations in the state. By appt. (318-379-2382).

CANE RIVER COUNTRY: the area south of Natchitoches along both sides of Cane River Lake is a scenic 53-mile loop. Cane River Lake was once part of the Red River. When the river changed its course, a long, narrow oxbow waterway was left, bordered by plantation homes and other historic development. Dams are at either end of the 32-mile-long lake. **Sang pour Sang** (blood for blood): the traditional site of a battle in 1732 between French troops from Fort St. Jean Baptiste in Natchitoches and their Indian allies who annihilated the Natchez Indian Tribe. Off La. 119 about 1 mile, behind the Emmanuel School Building, to the end of the steep bluff which overlooks the dry lake where the battle is said to have occurred.

The Bayou Folk Museum, located on Main St. (La. 495) in Cloutierville, is housed in a Louisiana raised-cottage built in the early 1800s of handhewn cypress, slave-made bricks, and bousillage construction, restored to the period when author Kate Chopin lived here. The museum contains mementos of her life in Cane River Country. On the grounds are a blacksmith shop, country doctor's office, and displays of local farm implements. Admission. Open Mon.-Sat., 9-5; Sun., 1-5. (318-379-2546 or 379-2233). **Cloutierville Heritage Festival** is held the Saturday before Labor Day and features entertainment, arts and crafts, and children's activities. **Magnolia Plantation,** on La. 119, built in 1868 on the foundation of an earlier home burned during the Civil War, retains the original outbuildings, including the only cotton press (which predated the cotton gin) in the United States still in its original location. Open daily, 1-4. Admission. (318-379-2221). **St. Augustine Catholic Church,** built by free persons of color in 1806, is open daily. Graves and tombs of early settlers on the grounds surrounding the church. **Melrose Plantation,** La. 119 at La. 493, is a unique complex of nine buildings, the oldest of which dates to 1796. The original main house, Yucca, was constructed of local materials. The African House, of Congo-style architecture, was built circa 1800 as a storehouse and jail. The Big House, constructed about 1833, is a Louisiana-style plantation house with twin hexagonal garçonnieres and a kitchen wing added later. Other buildings include the bindery, Ghana House, Writer's Cabin, Weaving House, barn, and the home of the late primitive artist, Clementine Hunter. The plantation was the home of Lyle Saxon and François Mignon and was visited by numerous writers and artists. Admission. Open daily, 12-4. Closed on major holidays. Hosts the annual Melrose Plantation Arts and Crafts Festival, second weekend in June. (318-379-0055 or 379-2431).

   Roubieu Plantation, circa 1830, is a two-story home with the first floor of handmade brick and the upper story of cypress. Private. Drive-by. **Oakland Plantation,** constructed in 1818 of cypress and bousillage, features a 10-foot-wide gallery and a private museum on the lower floor containing plantation tools and memorabilia. The setting for the Civil War movie *The Horse Soldiers*. Private. Drive-by. **Beau Fort Plantation,** on La. 494, built in 1790 of cypress and bousillage, features an 84-foot-long gallery across the front, and lovely gardens. Admission. Open daily, 1-4. Closed Thanksgiving, Christmas, New Year's Day, and July 4. (318-352-5340 or 352-9580). **Cherokee Plantation** is a raised cottage built before 1839 and is named for its prolific Cherokee roses. The original cabins and stables are on the grounds. Private. Drive-by. **Oaklawn Plantation,** built in 1840, is a raised cottage constructed of cypress beams, brick, and bousillage. Drive-by.

   NATIONAL FISH HATCHERY: on La. 1 south, a 20-tank aquarium containing the species of fish propagated at this hatchery, as well as other species. It is the only facility in the state that raises freshwater fish to stock lakes and rivers in Louisiana and southern Arkansas. Open daily 8-4.

   NATCHITOCHES: pronounced "nak-a-tish." The oldest permanent settlement in the Louisiana Purchase Territory was founded in 1714 by Louis Juchereau de St. Denis and called Fort St. Jean Baptiste. It was renamed for a tribe of Caddo Indians whose name meant "chinquapin eaters." The town was located just below the great logjam on the Red River, making it a trade and commerce center. When the river changed its course, Natchitoches stopped developing and was left with its charm intact, a mixture of French, Spanish, and Anglo-Saxon influences. The old section is designated a National Historic Landmark. **Natchitoches Parish Tourist Commission,** 781 Front Street, offers information, brochures, and maps, including walking and driving tours. Open Mon.-Sat., 9-5; Sun., 10-3. (318-352-8072). For information on special performances, events, and exhibits, contact the **City of Natchitoches Arts Council.** (318-357-3829)

   Riverfront Drive passes through the heart of the historic district. **Roque House,** on the riverfront, was built in French Colonial style, of cypress with bousillage fill, in the early 1800s and was moved to this site. Offices of Cane River Cruises and trolley tours. **Ducournau Square,** a block of early-19th-century buildings on Front Street, includes the Cloutier Town House, a restored residence furnished in the early Empire period with art from the Natchitoches area. The brick-paved courtyard is reached by a carriageway from the street. Open by appt. Admission. (318-352-5242). **Trinity Episcopal Church,** Second at Trudeau, was begun in 1857 but not completed until after the Civil War. The church's cornerstone was laid by the Fighting Bishop, Leonidas Polk. **Immaculate Conception Catholic Church,** Church at Second, was begun in 1856 and completed in the 1880s. It contains graves of former bishops and a spiral staircase with no center support. The Rectory, across the street from the church, was moved to Natchitoches in 1885 from New Orleans. **Old Courthouse,** Church at Second, was built in 1896, the second building on this site. A spiral staircase leads to the clock tower. **American Cemetery,** Demeziere at Second, contains many lost graves from the 1700s and marked tombs dating to the 1790s. **Old Seminary:** Bishop Martin Museum, east of Rectory Street, was built in 1853 and recently restored. It is the depository for early records and church artifacts. By appt. (318-352-2651). **Prudhomme-Rouquier House,** 436 Jefferson, one of the largest bousillage structures in the United States, was built before 1800 and remodeled circa 1830. By appt. (318-352-6723). **Lemee House,** 310 Jefferson, built in 1830, is a fine example of French Colonial style and has one of the first cellars in Natchitoches. Headquarters for Fall Tour of Historic Homes. By appt. (318-352-8072). **Wells House,** 607 Williams Avenue, is one of the oldest in the Mississippi Valley and reflects the 19th-century prosperity of the area. By appt. (318-352-2095). **Natchitoches Pilgrimage** (tour of homes) is held the second weekend in October and opens up many of the usually private town homes and buildings and Cane River plantations. Includes a candlelight tour. Admission. (There are many private houses designated on tourist maps not mentioned here that can be seen as drive-by or walk-by.)

Fort St. Jean Baptiste State Commemorative Area, Mill Street, is an exact replica of the fort used from 1715 to 1737 by the French and their Indian allies as protection against the Spanish and unfriendly Indian tribes. The replica is situated on the Cane River, a few hundred yards south of the original site and shows the barracks, warehouse, chapel, mess hall, and Indian huts as they appeared in 1732. Interpretive program. Open daily, 9-5. Admission. (318-357-3101). **Northwestern State University:** *Normal Hill,* the oldest part of the campus, is the most beautiful and historic. *The turn-of-the-century One Room School House* is one of the few extant. *Louisiana Room, Watson Library,* contains archives of the city and parish and district history. Open weekdays, 8-4. *The Williamson Museum,* in the Kyzar Arts and Sciences Building, contains significant collections and exhibits of Louisiana prehistory, Indian cultures, artifacts, and cultural history. Open weekday, Sept.-May, 8-4:30. *Louisiana Sports Hall of Fame,* Prather Coliseum, honors more than 60 of Louisiana's greatest sports figures. Open weekdays, 8-4:30. *The Louisiana School for Math, Science and the Performing Arts* is a model public residential high school for high-achieving students in grades 10, 11, and 12. *For information on special exhibits and performances on the campus of Northwestern State University, call 318-357-4522.*

Natchitoches Folk Festival, held in Prather Coliseum, is one of the most significant gatherings for the presentation of the rich and diverse folklife traditions of Louisiana, including Anglo-Saxon, Cajun, Creole, Indian, French, and Spanish. Music, crafts, food, entertainment. Second weekend in October. Admission. (318-357-4332). **Christmas Lights and Set Pieces** along the Cane River each evening from 5:30-11 P.M. from the first weekend in December through New Year. The Christmas Festival of Lights features parade, fireworks, food, and entertainment, and is held the first Saturday in December. **Sibley Lake,** west of Natchitoches, is a scenic spot for fishing and boating. Boat ramps. The Union troops occupied Natchitoches for 21 days in April 1864, as they massed for their push to capture Shreveport. Under Gen. Nathaniel Banks, Union troops destroyed the town of Grand Encore just 4 miles north of Natchitoches.

Unique Louisiana

EVERYTHING'S COMING UP ROSES

Multi-perfumed fragrances dance in the air over a landscape colored like an impressionist palette; a carillon windchime sings through the whisper of pines. It leads some to say that, between April and December, when the roses in the American Rose Center Garden burst into bloom, this swatch of land in northwest Louisiana seems much closer to heaven than to the Texas border.

But, indeed, the garden, along with the American Rose Society headquarters, is located on 118 gently rolling acres nudging the state line a mere ten miles west of Shreveport—a magnet to all who appreciate the radiance of planned and cultivated beauty.

The American Rose Society, the official organization of amateur rosarians (rose growers) since 1899, moved here from Columbus, Ohio, in 1974 after a generous donor offered the property. The Society furnishes information about every imaginable aspect of rose-growing, rose trivia (i.e., roses are the oldest plants known to man that can still be found in modern gardens), offers slide shows and publications, and conducts test gardening. A horticultural lending library and a gift shop specializing in merchandise with rose motifs share the headquarters building.

But most visitors come to stroll through more than forty intimate garden settings that display over 300 varieties of rose finery in disparate settings such as a Japanese landscape, around the tracing of intricate brickworks, on decorative patios with fountains, trellises, and gazebos, and in informal beds.

The gardens have each been planned and donated by a state rose society or in memory of a rosarian. New gardens are added regularly. And though roses dominate the landscape, azaleas, stately trees, annuals, and native plants add texture . . . and fill in when the stars of this flora park are off duty or out of season.

If maintaining a garden is demanding, maintaining a rose garden is the extreme, as the old adage would indicate: roses are so difficult, it is said, that no one can successfully raise both roses and children.

Indeed, each of the 20,000 rosebushes must be sprayed, pruned, and weeded weekly, watered weekly if too little rain has fallen, fertilized monthly, and always sufficiently mulched.

Which partially explains the evolution of the annual Pruning Day celebration—lovingly called the horticultural equivalent of a bass tournament—which takes place each February. Rosarians from all over the country arrive at the Gardens with their trowels and work-benches to clean up their society's plot, share rose tales, and socialize. It is merely serendipity that it gives the garden's staff a headstart on the season.

· Gardeners are always under strict orders to prune rosebushes carefully and to be alert for passing guests. For while visitors to the gardens are absolutely forbidden to pick the blossoms, it's an unwritten rule that gardeners are forbidden to throw a bloom away if it can be presented to a visiting rose-lover instead.

American Rose Society gardens, Shreveport. (Courtesy Louisiana Office of Tourism)

FISHER

Once-upon-a-time, at the turn of the century, a thriving mill town sprang up in west central Louisiana. Built entirely of wood taken from the vast pine forests that covered the surrounding hills, the Village of Fisher was the largest sawmill town in Sabine Parish—an impressive superlative considering the magnitude of the timber industry at the time.

Fisher was, by every definition, a company town, the creation and reflection of the 4L Company, as the Louisiana Long Leaf Lumber Company was nicknamed. 4L built and owned the mill and the entire village. Old timers whisper that when someone disregarded company regulations, he lost not only his job but had to give up his house and move away.

4L built Fisher thoughtfully. A wooden opera house, with velvet curtains, seats for 300 and a little standing room at the back by the Jewel, potbellied stove, hosted lively entertainment that made the frame of the structure rattle with joy.

The commissary first unlocked its glass doors in 1900, selling "general merchandise," according to its bold black sign. The merchandise and the prices were so good shoppers came all the way from Texas, across the Sabine River. The commissary had to be enlarged in 1914.

As the site of the most important sawmill on the Kansas City Southern Railway, Fisher also boasted a diminutive wooden depot just off the paved town plaza, where everyone shared community news and exchanged greetings. A rambling, wood-frame hotel next to 4L office headquarters, a post office, school, hospital, and, eventually, even a car dealership and a grocery made Fisher a near-metropolis.

Mill workers and their families lived in cottages made of pine; a few were precisely laid log cabins. The managers resided in comfortable, tree-shaded frame homes along a row nicknamed Silk Stocking Lane. The ladies visited from house to house, walking carefully along the wood plank sidewalks, or leaned across their neat picket fences to talk. Everything that could conceivably be made of wood was wooden; fire hydrants were strategically located.

Once-upon-a-time ended for the Village of Fisher in 1966 when new owners bought the sawmill and subdivided the model sawmill company town, selling it to the residents. Fisherites realized that theirs was a unique site, an unusual community in the twentieth century and, hoping to preserve it, organized the nonprofit Fisher Heritage Foundation, Inc.

In subsequent years, the railroad deeded the depot; the new mill owners donated the commercial center of town—9 1/2 acres that included the office, commissary, opera house, post office, and village square—and Fisher earned a designation as a Louisiana Landmark and a place on the National Register of Historic Districts. Sawmill Days, a festival celebrating Fisher's heyday and held annually on the fourth weekend in May, also was created.

But today, Sawmill Days is the only occasion when anything more than wind creaks the batten walls of the Opera House. Its potbellied stoves are cold; the velvet curtains are faded tan and ragged. A single strip of plank sidewalk outside the Opera House is all that's left, and the cavernous commissary is dim and empty, its shelves gaping in the expanse. The hotel site is a grassy, shaded lot; the car dealership, hospital, school, and grocery have been removed. No train stops at the depot and only the post office and the company office, used as town hall, seem quietly inhabited.

Fisher, like so many of Louisiana's unique places, is caught hanging between the vitality of its past and the promise of a future in which its colorful history could delight generations who would learn from it about a way of life long gone.

But for now, the Village of Fisher waits, like so many other places. And only those who share the memory of what it was and the hope of what it might be again will look for the unmarked turn-off on La. 171 and visit, before the promise is fulfilled . . . or the ravages of time destroy what's left.

3

Alexandria and Crosscurrents

Central Louisiana's asymmetrical geography is a perfect symbol for the state's heartland, the junction of cultures and traditions that ebb and flow through its midline, a transition from swamps to hills. South Louisiana's Cajun-French influence seeps north through Avoyelles Parish, blending with the Anglo-Saxon heritage that flows from the north. Plantation homes and Civil War history, Long family legends, French, Spanish, and Anglo-Saxon influences, technology, agriculture, and recreation all fuse to create lively crosscurrents in the area composed of Winn, Catahoula, Concordia, La Salle, Grant, Avoyelles, Rapides, and Vernon parishes. A portion of one of Louisiana's overland trails, followed during the 19th-century migration of westward settlers, 1803-50, crosses this area from Vidalia to Winnfield, continuing west to Toledo Bend. The largest city in central Louisiana is Alexandria.

KISATCHIE NATIONAL FOREST, WINN DISTRICT: Cloud Crossing, off La. 1233, marks the beginning of the cypress-lined Saline Bayou Canoe Trail. Camping, picnicking, bird-watching, boat launch. Gum Springs, U.S. 84, offers camping, picnicking, bird-watching. (See Chapter 2 for Readhimer area)

BACKWOOD VILLAGE INN: La. 126, west of Dodson, promotes local culture through a monthly Pioneer Day exhibit and demonstrations. (318-727-9227)

WINN PARISH DOGWOOD TRAIL: U.S. 84, 16 miles west of Winnfield, is a 1 1/2-mile hiking trail with numerous flowering trees and plants identified.

WINNFIELD: the birthplace of three legendary Louisiana governors, Huey P. Long, O. K. Allen, and Earl K. Long. Winnfield became

Alexandria Area

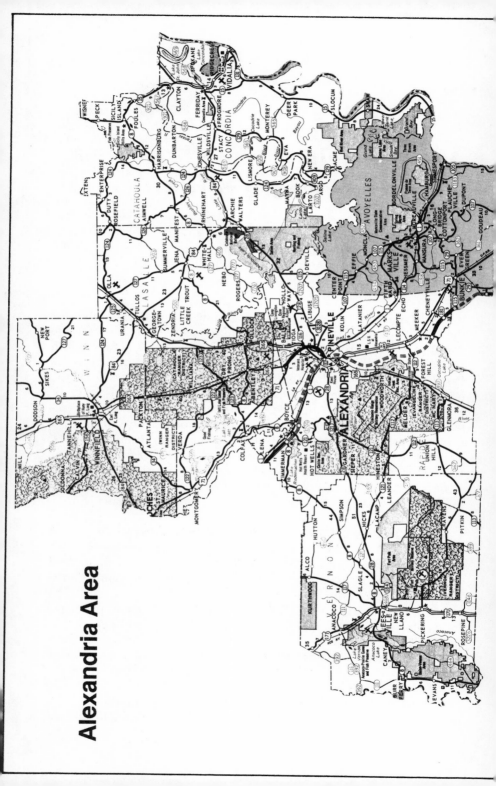

the Free State of Winn when it refused to secede from the Union with the rest of Louisiana. **Jones House,** 510 Jones Street, has incorporated the original one-room log courthouse for Winn Parish within its structure. **The Winnfield Hotel,** an impressive three-story built in 1908, is located at 302 E. Main. **George P. Long House**, built in 1905, 1401 Maple, is a Queen Anne Revival style home. Private. **The Louisiana Forest Festival** offers forestry events, equipment displays, arts and crafts, parade, and entertainment. Late April. In the one-acre **Earl K. Long Commemorative Area** are a statue and pavilion honoring Louisiana's first three-term governor and well-known character, Earl K. Long, younger brother of Huey Long. Picnicking. For Winn Parish tourist information, visit the Winnfield Chamber of Commerce, located in the courthouse. (318-628-4461)

ST. MAURICE: outside of this town on U.S. 71 are the ruins of St. Maurice Plantation, built in the classical style in 1840. Burned in 1981.

COOCHIE BRAKE: near Atlanta, off La. 34, is a near-wilderness area of 700 acres of creeks, boulders, caves, and tunnels that reputedly served as the hideout for the Kimbrell gang of robbers in the 1870s.

LAKE IATT AND LAKE NANTACHES: located off U.S. 71 north of Colfax, offer excellent fishing, boat rentals, and launch. A game and fish preserve are at Lake Iatt.

COLFAX: the seat of Grant Parish was named after Ulysses S. Grant's vice-president, Schuyler Colfax, and was a trouble spot during Reconstruction. In the downtown district are several significant turn-of-the-century buildings including the LeSage Hotel, and McNeely House. **The Louisiana Pecan Festival** features pioneer dress, turkey shoot, arts and crafts, and entertainment, first weekend in November.

KISATCHIE NATIONAL FOREST, CATAHOULA DISTRICT: The Catahoula National Wildlife Management Preserve, within the boundaries of the national forest, offers year-round fishing and seasonal hunting with special hunting programs and education. Stuart Lake, off La. 8 near Pollock, offers camping, amenities, and an interpretive trail. Primitive camping in the national forest is allowed at Saddle Bayou, off Forest Service Road 155; at Pearson (within the national management preserve); and at Bankston, off Forest Road 145. The Grant Parish Dogwood Trail, Forest Road 120, is a 10-mile interpretive auto tour, especially beautiful in the spring.

POLLOCK: host to the **Shady Dell Bluegrass Festival,** with extensive campsite facilities and limited hook-ups. First weekend in May; last weekend in Sept. Admission. (318-765-9092)

KITTERLING BAY, LEYMAN'S LAKE, WALTER LAKE: east of

Pollock, this area offers good fishing, hunting, hiking, canoeing, camping. Boat rentals, launch, bait and tackle.

WHITE SULPHUR SPRINGS: La. 8, 11 miles northeast of Pollock, was a fancy resort noted for the healing powers of its waters in the mid-19th century. Gambling, champagne dances, and other entertainments prevailed. Though the Louisiana Board of Health in 1911 declared the waters powerless, legends survive about their extraordinary curative powers. Area now has walkways, footbridge, picnic area, and covered gazebo to represent its former glory.

LITTLE RIVER-CATAHOULA LAKE: off La. 28, offers camping, fishing, hunting, hiking, boat launch and rentals. Indian Bluff, a 3-acre site, overlooks the lake from the end of La. 777.

SALINE WILDLIFE MANAGEMENT AREA: access off La. 128, a tract of over 60,000 acres with excellent fishing, hunting, and 4 camping areas, 3 with water and restrooms. (318-757-4571). Saline Bayou, off La. 28, is a facility for camping, fishing, hunting, canoeing, biking, boat launch and rental.

LARTO LAKE: 8 miles south of Jonesville off La. 24. Hunting, picnicking, and swimming. Good fishing; guide recommended. **NEBO:** Mt. Nebo Baptist Church, founded in 1855, was dissolved and reorganized in 1891. A school district that was the first in Louisiana to vote taxes to support its schools was later added.

JENA: the town's early history is intertwined with that of the Choctaw, Natchez, and Avoyel Indians. The Jena Choctaw tribe Indian Center, corner La. 459 and Coward Street, exhibits traditional artifacts and crafts. **Eden Methodist Church,** believed to be the oldest Methodist church south of the Mason-Dixon line, has records dating to its founding in 1778. Located on La. 8, 3 miles south of Jena. **Summerfest,** held the first weekend in June in the park, features crafts, entertainment, games and contests, and food. For LaSalle Parish tourist information, inquire at the LaSalle Development Board, at the courthouse, or call (318) 992-4441.

GOODPINE: LaSalle Parish Museum, on U.S. 84. Located in a lumber company headquarters, built in 1906. Exhibits local crafts and historical memorabilia. Wed., 1-4; Thurs., 9-4. Groups by appt. (318-992-8351)

OLLA: first known as Sulphur Springs, the town was a steamboat landing on Castor Creek during the 19th century.

TULLOS: legends have it that the explorer LaSalle smoked a peace pipe with an important Choctaw chief here and that the famed Natchez Treasure containing lumps of silver and sacks of gold is buried nearby. The town is named for Joe Tullos, its founder, to whom a monument stands near the New Union Baptist Church. Now a nearly deserted oil boom town.

THE DUTY FERRY: located at Enterprise, this small boat has plied the Ouachita River for as long as anyone can remember, carrying one or two cars at a time. Local color. (Schedule erratic.)

CATAHOULA BAPTIST CHURCH: near Enterprise. Founded circa 1825, this rough-hewn, simple structure is considered the mother church of central Louisiana. The cemetery contains century-old graves with unusual headstones. Memorial Day services held on the second Sunday in May.

ROCK CANYON: off La. 126 in the pine hills lies this horseshoe-shaped canyon with large boulders and a tall waterfall. The Rock Canyon Trail traces the bluff. In late March and early April, when dogwood and other native shrubs are in bloom, the trail is called the Catahoula Dogwood Trail. **At Lakewood Park,** on a pine-forested bluff overlooking a rippling, boulder-strewn stream, is a walking and picnic area and a gazebo.

AIMWELL: Old McGuffie Homestead, an 1870s wooden farmhouse, is the focal point of this working farm offering live local entertainment on weekends.

FORT BEAUREGARD: La. 124 north of Harrisonburg. Originally called Fort Hill, this military post, constructed in 1862, was renamed in honor of Gen. P. G. T. Beauregard. Destroyed in 1863. Battlepark Festival, a reenactment of the August 1863 battle, takes place the first weekend in November (318-435-9238). **Harrisonburg Methodist Church,** built in the mid-19th century, stands with bullet scars from the Civil War and a picturesque cemetery. Near Old Fort Beauregard.

Fort Hill Park adjoins the site of Fort Beauregard. It is a Civil War recreational and entertainment theme park overlooking the Ouachita River and featuring an outdoor amphitheatre for live performances, entertainment, and a heritage and cultural compound. Park headquarters is a Civil War era post office building moved from Harrisonburg. For more information, call (318) 744-5397.

HARRISONBURG: Indians and early settlers in this area developed the breed of dog now known as the Catahoula Cur. Catahoula is an Indian word for "clear water" or "beloved lake." **Sargeant House,** on Catahoula Street, is a story-and-a-half cottage, originally used as a hotel for steamboat passengers prior to 1910. By appt. **The Catahoula Parish Museum of Natural History,** housed in the Catahoula Parish Courthouse, contains an excellent collection of Indian artifacts—some prehistoric—a model of the Troyville Mound, and exhibits of area history and memorabilia. Open weekdays, 8-4:30. For area tourist information call (318) 339-7898.

BUSHLEY BAYOU: south of Harrisonburg, off La. 923. Legendary frontiersman Jim Bowie lived and developed his famed knife here.

JONESVILLE: believed to be the Indian village "Anilco" to which DeSoto referred in 1541. Four rivers—the Little, Tensas, Ouachita, and Black—meet near **Jonesville Riverfront Park,** north of Jonesville. **The Great Mound,** a sacred prehistoric Indian ceremonial site, covered what is now Jonesville, La. 8 at La. 24. It was gradually demolished as the town expanded, and the artifacts found there are now at the Smithsonian Institution in Washington, D.C. **King Turtle Farm** offers tours of a commercial turtle producer, except in May and June when the turtles are laying eggs. **The Catahoula Soybean Festival** features exhibits, pageant, ball, and agricultural exhibits the second weekend in September. **The Jonesville Historical Marker,** at U.S. 84 and La. 124, relates DeSoto's final battle in 1542 and the story of the Natchitoches-Natchez Road. **Catahoula Tourist Commission,** 106 Jasmine. (318-339-8498)

SICILY ISLAND: local legend suggests the town was named for an early settler who was reminded of the topography of his native country. In the late 19th century, Russian Jews attempted to establish an agricultural community, but few of them were farmers and the settlement failed. Cotton remains an important agricultural product. **Battleground Plantation** (La. 15 north), circa 1830, retains much of its beautiful original woodwork. Open by appt. **Peck Gin** and **Yarborough Gin** are two steam-powered cotton gins, still in use, that date from the early 1900s. **Ferry Plantation** (west of Sicily Island off La. 1017), built in the late 18th century, is a gracious, two-story home overlooking Lake Louie. Open by appt. **Pine Hill Plantation** (west of Sicily Island, off La. 913), is a West Indies-style house built 1820-23. Open by appt. (For Battleground, Ferry, and Pine Hill, call 318-389-5750.) **Green Lovelace** (La. 15 north of Sicily Island) is a raised wood cottage with unusual fanlights. Drive-by. **Frontier Days,** held July 4 weekend, features a parade, crafts and booths, entertainment, and folk music and dance. (318-389-5683)

SICILY ISLAND HILLS WILDLIFE MANAGEMENT AREA: located 6 miles west of Sicily Island, off La. 8 and 915, this 6,000-acre tract contains rugged terrain with high ridges dropping to creek bottoms. Hunting and permit trapping available, as well as fishing during high water in the Boeuf and Ouchita rivers. Primitive camping. Trail to scenic waterfall and creek. (318-757-4571)

LAKE CONCORDIA: east of U.S. 65 near Ferriday. A 1,000-acre, scenic oxbow trophy-bass lake offering fishing, boating, skiing, sailing, and camping.

FERRIDAY: located on the historic Nolan's Trace, one of the Texas-bound trails blazed by Philip Nolan in the late 18th century. Nolan was a pioneer horse trader who was captured and put to death in 1801 for contraband trading with the Americans at Natchez and the Spanish in Texas. Edward Everett Hale immortalized him as "the man without a country." Tourism information (318-757-4297). Ferriday is the birthplace of newscaster Howard K. Smith and three famous cousins—entertainers Mickey Gilley and Jerry Lee Lewis and televangelist Jimmy Swaggart. Lisburne Plantation, off La. 3196, built in 1852, is an outstanding example of a Greek Revival style raised plantation home. Drive-by.

FROGMORE: site of the 8-foot-high Frogmore Indian Mound, a prehistoric mound easily visible from U.S. 84. **Frogmore Cotton Gin** is open for tours during cotton harvest, in late fall.

VIDALIA: the town is the site of the first Spanish post of Concord in 1798 and later an important steamboat town at the east end of the Texas Cattle Trail. Vidalia was the origination of the Louisiana portion of the colonial trail in 1830. **Louisiana Tourist Information Center,** U.S. 84. Information, maps, and brochures. Open weekdays, 8:30-5. (318-336-7008). **Taconey Plantation,** on U.S. 84 west, is one of the few remaining antebellum homes in the region and the only brick structure. Taconey was one of the top cotton-producing plantations before the Civil War. By appt. Site of the annual Jim Bowie Festival.

BLACK RIVER AND BLACK RIVER LAKE: south of Jonesville, off La. 600. The area has fishing, canoeing, hunting, camping, boat rental and launch.

RED RIVER WILDLIFE MANAGEMENT AREA: access from La. 15 and La. 910. 28,000-acre tract for hunting, trapping by permit, fishing, bird-watching, camping, comfort station. (318-757-4571)

THREE RIVERS WILDLIFE MANAGEMENT AREA: access from La. 15 and La. 910. This almost-24,000-acre tract located between the Mississippi and Red rivers, just north of Lower Old River, offers hunting, fishing, trapping by permit, wildlife-viewing, campsite, waterwells, and comfort stations. (318-575-4571)

OLD RIVER NAVIGATION LOCK: off La. 15. An impressive structure, part of the Mississippi River and Tributaries Project for flood control, designed to keep the Mississippi on its present course and prevent its natural tendency to switch channels into the Atchafalaya River. A low sill structure operates at all times to regulate normal flow, and an overbank structure operates in high water.

MURRAY HYDRO-ELECTRIC PLANT: the first hydro-electric power plant in the state, located next to the Old River Control Structure. Tours of the facility available. (318-336-9666)

GRASSY LAKE WILDLIFE MANAGEMENT AREA: off La. 451. Rough access to 12,000 acres in the Red River flood plain. Smith Bay, Grassy Lake, and Lake Chenier provide good fishing; the hardwood forest cover offers hunting, trapping by permit. Primitive camping. (318-942-7553)

SIMMESPORT: located near the junction of the Red, Atchafalaya, and Old rivers, the town is enclosed by a levee. The point at which the Red joins the Mississippi is said to be DeSoto's burial place. Simmesport, in Avoyelles Parish, was inhabited by Napoleon's soldiers rather than by Acadian French. **Yellow Bayou Civil War Memorial Park** commemorates the last battle of General Banks' Red River Campaign in 1864. Picnic and recreational facilities. (318-941-2493)

MOREAUVILLE: the village, off La. 1 at one end of historic Bayou des Glaises, was settled in the early 19th century. Several historic sites are private—drive-by only: **Sacred Heart Catholic Church,** second oldest in the parish; Boyer Home, circa 1840; Paradise Plantation, circa 1941; Couvillion Home, circa 1900; Lemoine Home, circa 1910.

HAMBURG: La. 1 at La. 451, named, according to local legend, by German laborers. **Calliham Plantation,** circa 1841, the only antebellum home in the area, and **Mayfield,** circa 1885, Louisiana Georgian style. Drive-by. **Mayfield**, an Italianate planter's home built circa 1885, was moved from Moreauville in 1978. Drive-by.

POMME DE TERRE WILDLIFE MANAGEMENT AREA: off La. 451 by gravel road. A 6,000-acre tract for hunting, trapping by permit. Sutton Lake is the principal fishing area, with boat ramp and primitive camping. (318-942-7553)

SPRING BAYOU WILDLIFE MANAGEMENT AREA: 3 miles east of Marksville. Over 12,000 acres of poorly drained Red River backwater offers trapping by permit, hunting, excellent fishing, 3 camping areas, and boat ramps. (318-253-7068.)

MANSURA: headquarters for the annual Avoyelles Tour of Homes, first week in October. (318-964-2054). **Historic Downtown Mansura,** La. 107 and L'Eglise Street, exhibits a variety of historic and architecturally significant buildings from the late 18th century to the early 20th century. **Defossé House,** built circa 1796, a Louisiana French Colonial construction of bousillage-entre-poteau, has been restored and furnished to its mid-19th-century period. Tues.-Sat., 11-3 or by appt. (318-964-2887)

MARKSVILLE: established by the Spanish in 1783 as Poste de

Avoyelles, the town was settled by French Acadian exiles and named for French trader Mark Eliche. **Hypolite Bordelon House** is a Creole dwelling built during 1800 to 1820 with bousillage-entre-poteau construction. It houses the **Marksville Tourist Center,** open Tues.-Sat., 11-3, or by appt. (318-253-7047). Also headquarters for the annual **Cochon de Lait Festival** held in mid-April. The Arts & Humanities Council of Avoyelles offers information on special exhibits, performances, and events. (318-253-5511). **The Marksville Downtown Historic District,** dominated by the neoclassical courthouse building erected in 1927, contains many late-19th-and early-20th-century structures, both residential and commercial. **Tunica-Biloxi Regional Indian Center and Museum** on La. 1 houses the Tunica treasure, a collection of Indian and European artifacts from the colonial period. Open Tues.-Sat., 8-4. (318-253-8174). **Easter Egg Knocking Festival,** held Easter Sunday in Courthouse Square.

    MARKSVILLE (STATE) COMMEMORATIVE AREA: adjacent to the town of Marksville, east of La.1 and La. 452, is this important archeological site and ceremonial mounds where a prehistoric Indian culture lived from1to 400 A.D. Museum and interpretive program. Open daily, 9-5. Admission. (318-853-9546)

    EVERGREEN: Bayou Rouge Baptist Church, built in 1859, is an example of Greek Revival country churches commonly found in the state's eastern rural parishes before the Civil War. La. 29 east of U.S. 71.

    BUNKIE: the site of **Epps House** (Main Street), built in 1853, which figured prominently in Solomon Northup's book *Twelve Years a Slave.* It was moved to its present location to serve as the **Bunkie Tourist Information Center** for the area. (318-346-2575). **The Northup Trail,** tracking the history of Solomon Northup, runs from Bunkie through Evergreen and north to Marksville.

    CHENEYVILLE: plantation houses face Bayou Boeuf, so named because a boatload of cattle (*boeuf* in French) sank in the bayou near here. **Beulah Baptist Church,** founded in 1816, is the second oldest church west of the Mississippi River. The balcony was reserved for slaves of the white members, who sat on the first floor. Cemetery. **Trinity Episcopal Church,** built in 1860, located on Bayou Boeuf, has its original furnishings, with the slave gallery above the vestibule. Open daily. **Loyd Hall,** a three-story, brick-and-plaster classic-revival plantation house built in 1810, was used by both Confederate and Union troops. Its owner was hanged as a Confederate spy. Open Tues.-Sat., 10-4; Sun., 1-4. Admission. (318-776-5641). **Walnut Grove Plantation House,** built in 1840, belongs to members of the original family. Several outbuildings are on the grounds of this Greek Revival home. Open Tues.-Sun., 1-4. Admission. (318-279-2203). **The Cedars,** constructed in 1830, is a typical working plantation home that was won in a Mississippi riverboat card game and has been lived in by members of the family ever since. By appt. (318-279-2470). **Producer's Mutual Cotton Gin**, U.S. 71, conducts tours. Open Mon.-Wed. and Fri., 9-3. Ginning season Sept. through Nov. (318-279-2145). **Cheneyville Tour of Historic Places,** the third weekend in May, features tours of historic homes and churches, arts and crafts show, food, and entertainment. Admission. (318-279-2470)

LECOMPTE: Indian Creek Lake, near Lecompte, east of U.S. 165, is a 2,200-acre lake with part open for skiing. Boat launch, floating dock, nature trails, sand beaches, and camping. **St. John Baptist Church,** off La. 457 near Lecompte, a fine example of Queen Anne style, was organized in 1869 for the black residents of Ashton Plantation.

KOLIN: located on La. 107, is the site of a Czechoslovakian community that hosts an annual Czech Heritage Day Festival in March, featuring cultural exhibits, arts and crafts, food, and tours. Call Rapides Parish Convention and Visitors Bureau for information. (318-443-9513)

ALEXANDRIA/PINEVILLE: the area was called Les Rapides in French and El Rapido by the Spanish because of a limestone ledge that created a rapids in the Red River at high water, forcing river traffic to stop and navigate around it. Alexander Fulton laid out Alexandria in what was predominantly Indian territory in 1805. Settlers with Spanish land grants collected nearby, along bayous Rapides, Boeuf, and Roberts. Businesses developed for transporting steamboat cargo around the rapids. During the Civil War, the rapids stymied the Federal invasion and, after the defeat at Mansfield, retreating Union soldiers burned Alexandria, destroying much of the city.

Rapides Parish Convention and Tourist Bureau: located at 2020 W. MacArthur (behind the white teepee by the north traffic circle). Tourist information, maps, brochures. Open Mon.-Fri., 8-5; Sat., 9-4. (318-443-9513). **The Rapides Arts and Humanities Council** offers information on special exhibits, performances, and events. (318-443-ARTS). **St. Francis Xavier Cathedral,** Fourth at Beauregard, is a Gothic-style church built in 1898 at the site of a mutiny of troops under the command of Gen. George Armstrong Custer. Open daily. **Alexandria Museum,** 933 Main in a former bank building, houses a permanent collection as well as travelling exhibits. Open Tues.-Fri., 9-5; Sat., 10-4. Admission. (318-443-3458). **Bentley Hotel,** 801 Third

Street, is a renovated, neoclassical building built in 1908, restored to its original beaux-arts interior, with marble columns, gilded ceilings, and velvet furnishings in the public room. **River Oaks Arts and Crafts Center,** 1330 Main Street, is located in a turn-of-the-century home and features local artists working in their media. Open Tues.-Sat., 10-5. (318-473-2670). **Alexandria Historical and Genealogical Library/Museum,** housed in a library built in 1907 at Washington and Fifth streets. Open Tues.-Sat., 10-4. **Alexandria Zoological Park** in Bringhurst Park contains a zoo with over 400 animals, including endangered species, large cat exhibit, and waterfowl collection. Open 9-5 daily. Admission.

James C. Bolton Library at LSU-Alexandria exhibits work of regional and local artists. Open Mon.-Fri., 8-4:30; Sat., 8:30-12:30. **Kent House,** 3601 Bayou Rapides Road, built in 1796 in French and Spanish Colonial architecture, is the oldest building extant in central Louisiana. The 4-acre property also includes a variety of outbuildings — kitchen, slave cabins, barn, carriage house, and milkhouse. On La. 496. Open Mon.-Sat., 9-5; Sun., 1-4. Open-hearth cooking demos Wednesday mornings from October to April. Admission. (318-487-5998). **Tyrone Plantation,** on Bayou Rapides, was built in 1846 by Gen. George Mason Graham. **Cenlabration,** a celebration of levee living and life in Central Louisiana, takes place near the Red River in downtown Alexandria Labor Day weekend. Arts and crafts, music, street dancing, food. Free. (318-443-7039). **Rosalie Sugar Mill,** off U.S. 71 south on Bayou Robert, is the only surviving regional example of early American agricultural architecture, with handhewn cypress beams and handmade bricks. Started in 1845, the mill is no longer open but can be seen by driving by. **Inglewood Plantation,** with one of the last remaining sharecropper's warehouses, is a working cotton plantation, also on Bayou Robert. Private. Drive-by. A scenic drive along La. 121 from Alexandria to Boyce offers views of historic homes. Drive-by.

PINEVILLE: located just across the Red River from Alexandria, Pineville is the site of Fort Buhlow and Fort Randolph, built on either side of the Pineville Bridge to repel Union troops. The forts were never used and nothing remains. At the Fort Buhlow site is a picnic grounds; adjacent Lake Buhlow offers fishing, boating, and swimming; the national championship power boat races are held on Lake Buhlow annually. **Bailey's Dam,** site of the dam constructed by Federal troops during the Civil War to move their gunboats over the rapids, is marked near the O. K. Allen Bridge. The old Louisiana State University site off U.S. 71 is the original home of LSU, opened in 1860 under headmaster William Tecumseh Sherman. The college was closed during the Civil War, but reopened in 1865, only to burn in 1869. The campus was then moved to Baton Rouge. Brick foundations are left at the site, which is just north of the Alexandria Forestry Center. **Kees Park,** on La. 28, features swimming, picnicking, playground, and civic center. **The Catahoula Lake Festival** is celebrated here the last weekend in October, with heritage activities such as duck decoy carving, spinning, weaving, and featuring the Catahoula Cur. **Mt. Olivet Church,** on Main Street, was dedicated in 1854 and was used by Union soldiers during their occupation. **Pineville National Cemetery,** on U.S. 165, was established in 1867 and contains graves from the Indian, Mexican, Civil, Spanish-American, and World wars.

ALEXANDER FOREST WILDLIFE MANAGEMENT AREA: near Woodworth off U.S. 165 is a 7,800-acre recreational area with camping, picnicking, and swimming in a large lake and a special area for hunting. Admission. (318-487-5885)

INDIAN CREEK RECREATION AREA: off U.S. 165, includes a 2,250-acre lake, partly open for skiing. Boat launch, floating dock, camping, nature trails, sand beaches, and play areas. (318-445-2933)

KISATCHIE NATIONAL FOREST, EVANGELINE DISTRICT: Kincaid Reservoir, off La. 28, has facilities for waterskiing, and a scenic 10-mile lakeside hiking trail. **Valentine Lake,** off gravel road 282, offers camping, picnicking, nature trail, swimming, restrooms, and facilities for handicapped. **Evangeline Lake,** off gravel road 273, has primitive camping, water, restrooms. **Castor Creek Scenic Area** features large pine, gum, ash, and other trees and is the start of the **Wild Azalea Trail,** a 30-mile, popular backpacking and hiking area. (318-445-9396)

COTILE LAKE RECREATION AREA: its manmade 400-acre lake offers picnicking, camping, sailing, boating, skiing. **Cotile Trade Days,** the last weekend in March, features two days of swapping of merchandise, animals, antiques, etc.

BOYCE: originally called Cotile Landing, this town was a shipping point for cattle driven in from Texas. The road to Boyce follows the levee on Bayou Jean de Jean, which was once a great river.

KISATCHIE NATIONAL FOREST, VERNON DISTRICT: Fullerton Lake, site of one of the largest early-20th-century sawmills. Offers fishing, picnicking, camping, bird-watching, nature trails. (318-239-6576)

FORT POLK: established in 1940 as a training camp for soldiers, named for Leonidas K. Polk, the famed "Fighting Bishop." The military post has seen service by generals Polk, Dwight Eisenhower, Omar

Bradley, Mark Clark, and George Patton. **The Fort Polk Military Museum** (Bldg. 17, S. Carolina Avenue) displays equipment, vehicles, flags, and uniforms dating to the American Revolution but specializing in military from World War II, 5th Infantry. Open Wed.-Fri., 10-2; weekends, 9-4. Free. Enter La. 467, just north of La. 10. (318-531-7905).

   NEW LLANO: on U.S. 171 south of Leesville, this cooperative colony was established in 1917 as a utopian community. Abandoned in 1935 but now established as a town.

   LEESVILLE: founded in 1871 and named for Robert E. Lee. **Vernon Parish Tourist Commission,** U.S. 171, is open weekdays, 8-12, 1-4. (318-238-0783). **The Vernon Arts Council** offers information on special exhibits, performances, and events. (318-239-2140). **Vernon Parish Courthouse,** built in 1910, is a neoclassical stucco structure with a cupola on a landscaped town square. **The Museum of West Louisiana,** 801 S. 3rd Street, in the renovated Railroad Depot, houses Vernon Parish memorabilia, railroad artifacts, and exhibits of Vernon Parish history. Open Tues.-Sun., 1-5. (318-239-0927). **Wingate House,** 400 S. 8th Street, is a 1905 Queen Anne revival-style house. By appt. Admission. (318-238-5142). **West Louisiana Forestry Festival,** end of Sept.

   LAKE ANACOCO: La. 8 and La. 464, offers fishing, swimming, boat launches, cottages.

   BOISE-VERNON WILDLIFE MANAGEMENT AREA: La. 464. Over 54,000 acres for hunting, trapping by permit, bird-watching, camping. (318-487-5885)

   BURR FERRY BREASTWORKS: La. 8. A small fenced park containing a portion of the Civil War redoubt erected by the Confederates to block an anticipated Union advance on the Sabine River. Undergoing restoration.

   LAKE VERNON: off La. 8 west, this small manmade lake offers fishing, boat launch, swimming, campsites.

   ANACOCO: Holly Grove Methodist Church, 4 miles south of town on U.S. 171 is a small frame structure built in 1834, the oldest in the parish and one of the oldest Protestant churches in the Louisiana Purchase. Still in use.

   PEASON RIDGE WILDLIFE MANAGEMENT AREA: owned by the U.S. Army, located in Vernon, Natchitoches, and Sabine parishes. This 33,000-acre tract of hilly pine woods offers permit hunting and trapping. No camping. (318-487-5885)

   SABINE RIVER: just below the Toledo Bend Dam (see northwest Louisiana for Toledo Bend information). For nearly 50 miles is considered an excellent canoeists' channel, with scenic areas, beaches, and take-out points. Some rock shoals. **Great Mother's Day Canoe Race,** from Toledo Bend Dam to Burr Ferry Bridge on La. 8.

CATAHOULA HOUND

Lassie was a collie, Rin-Tin-Tin a German Shepherd. Jack London immortalized a wild dog who was tamed and a domestic dog who escaped to lead a wolf pack, and a country mongrel named Old Yeller has become an American legend. But the Louisiana Catahoula Dog is still waiting for a little recognition, much less anything like full-blown celebrity status.

Just as the pelican is the official state bird and the magnolia the chosen state flower, the Louisiana Legislature recognized the state's only native domestic canine as the official state dog in 1979.

It was a worthy distinction. But while everyone calls a pelican a pelican and a magnolia a magnolia, the state dog is known by a variety of names—Catahoula Leopard Dog, Catahoula Cur, Catahoula Hound, Catahoula Hog Dog, and Catahoula Cow Dog, which, of course, indicates an obvious identity problem.

It's unfortunate, too, that the word "ugly" is the first response from strangers who are asked what they think of the athletic, oddly marked canine. Though the Catahoula's appearance may fall outside of the traditional definition of canine beauty, many of these spotted, splotched, and patchy-hided hounds are as appealing-looking as Benji, minus the whiskers. And, unlike most breeds whose coloration is predictably uniform within a narrow range of hues, the Catahoula's muscular body can be covered by the equivalent of a short-haired Joseph's coat—combinations of several of a variety of colors, including blue, gray, black, liver, red, white, tan, buff, black, brown, and yellow, with leopard spots part of the pattern. But not always.

A Catahoula gazes fondly at its master with a pair of milky-white eyes that often look, to the uninformed, glassy and spectral, even menacing—the eyes of the monster dog in teen horror movies. But the eyes, like the coat, may vary. A Catahoula Cur, as the National Association of Louisiana Catahoulas (NALC) refers to them, may have two white eyes, or two amber, green, brown, or glass-cracked eyes, or two unmatching eyes in not necessarily compatible colors. According

63

to NALC, however, the "Cadillac" of Catahoulas—the best of the breed—is "a big-boned, glass-eyed, white-trimmed blue leopard."

Certain characistics do supercede the differences, however, distinguishing pure Catahoulas from other breeds: webbed toes, for example, enable the dogs to walk easily through the swamp, and to swim well; an instinctive ability to trail silently and bay up only after locating prey, unlike other hunting dogs that bark along the trail; a working style somewhat akin to that of a champion prizefighter—darting, ducking, attacking, whirling, aggressive, savvy, hedging, and, ultimately, victorious; and a notorious loyalty to their owners.

This remarkable configuration of a dog was first discovered, or bred, or evolved, near Harrisonburg and Catahoula Lake, in the area now identified as Catahoula and LaSalle parishes. Its history mingles fact with legend, but the most widely espoused version of the Catahoula Cur's origins suggests that Hernando deSoto's war dogs, arriving with the explorer in 1542, encountered the local Indian dogs, or red wolves, and crossbred. The journals of LaSalle's Mississippi River expedition 140 years later make note of dogs with "white eyes and mottled spots." When the first white settlers arrived in the Catahoula Lake area during the eighteenth century, they were startled, then delighted, by the strange-looking dogs that were being used to hunt deer, bobcat, and wild hogs. The settlers called them *"catahoul"*—Indian for "clear water"—and trained them to help herd cattle as well as to hunt. In recent history, Jim Bowie owned Catahoulas, as did governors Huey and Earl Long. President Teddy Roosevelt hunted with one when he came to Louisiana.

While that may be the extent of their fame, it isn't because the NALC isn't trying. The current epicenter of Catahoula dog activity has moved from Catahoula Lake to Denham Springs, where the nonprofit organization has been headquartered since just after World War II at the instigation of one dedicated man who feared Catahoulas' extinction because of interbreeding. He worked to identify and preserve the breed. Today, breeders are found in many areas, and Louisiana Catahoula Curs are registered and living in almost every state and a few foreign countries, where they herd cattle, hunt deer, squirrel, hogs, and coon, and/or serve as house pets and family guardians.

And even to the uninformed, there is a certain appeal when a friendly Catahoula, with an expression of happiness in his pale eyes, sidles up, waving his tail like a curved baton leading a polka and causing the whole of his multicolored body to shiver and squirm with joy. He's a beautiful animal.

And the fact that he can trace his ancestry back to DeSoto should go a long way toward improving his social standing, too.

Catahoula hounds, Louisiana's official state dog. (Courtesy Louisiana Office of Tourism)

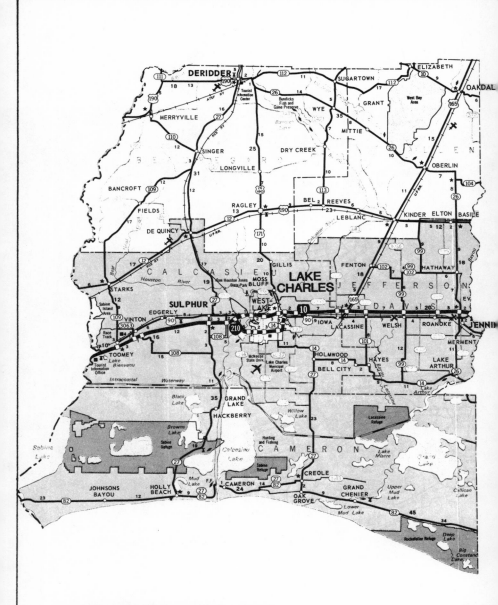

Lake Charles Area

4

Lake Charles
and the Southwest

The parishes of Beauregard, Allen, Calcasieu, Jefferson Davis, and Cameron comprise the area known to early French settlers as "Imperial Calcasieu." In this flat land of fishing, hunting, alligators, oil, and agriculture, at the western end of Louisiana's portion of the Intracoastal Waterway, the Cajun (French-Acadian) culture is a traditional influence and Lake Charles is the largest city. Much of the area, especially toward the coast, is a virtual bird-watchers'paradise due to its location on the southern end of the Mississippi Flyway.

DERIDDER: located on the site of a former Indian settlement. The **Beauregard Tourist Commission,** at 624 High School Drive in West Park, offers tourist information and brochures 8-4 weekdays. (318-463-5534). **Beauregard Museum,** in an old railroad depot at 120 S. Washington, exhibits antiques, pictures, and documents of the area from the early 1900s. Free. Open Tues.-Fri., 1-4. (318-463-5534). **The Beauregard Parish Jail** (Courthouse Square), built in 1914, is the most unusual jail in the state, with its Gothic styling and jail cells arranged around a monumental central tower. The turn-of-the-century **Historic Downtown DeRidder,** a National Register Historic District, features classic ornate architecture dating from 1880 to 1930. **The Beauregard Parish Fair**, first long weekend in October, features music, live entertainment, exhibits, and carnival.

MERRYVILLE: the site of an 18th-century Coushatta Indian village. Leatherbritches, a famed desperado known for the Graybow Mill shootout, is buried here. **The Burk Log Cabin (1883) and Museum** show historic artifacts of early settlers to the area. Open Thurs., Sat., Sun., 2-4. (318-825-8083). **Old Merryville Jail**built in 1912 housed the first union strikers in the United States in 1914. Several other turn-of-the-century homes are of interest. **Merryville Civil War enactment** is held the last weekend in February.

SUGARTOWN: the **Pine Grove Methodist Church Cemetery** features shelters (not burial tombs) over the graves as protection from the area's wild hogs. **Old Campground Cemetery** was first used in the 1820s. There is a replica of an original meetinghouse and a 1-mile nature trail along Sugar Creek. **Bluegrass Get Togethers,** second weekend in April and October at nearby Crooked Creek, offer music and camping.

WHISKEY CHITTO: one of the state's designated scenic waterways, which meanders through woodlands. Good bird-watching, canoeing, camping.

DRY CREEK: La. 113, is a pioneer community with an imposingly columned country school, now used as a church camp with a museum open to visitors on request. (318-328-7531)

BUNDICK LAKE: on La. 394, a 1,700-acre spring-fed lake known for excellent fishing. Fish and game preserve; swimming, boat launch, and camping facilities.

SINGER: a marker on La. 27 just north of Singer marks the route of the Old Confederate Military Road from Niblett's Bluff to Alexandria in 1862.

ELIZABETH: established as a lumber town in 1907 by Col. Sam Parks and Newton R. Wilson and named for Parks' daughter. The first Boy Scout troop in Louisiana began in this community. **Elizabeth Town Hall,** once the local hospital, is on the National Register. Christmas in the Country Festival in early December includes a parade, arts and crafts, horsemen's trail ride, music. (318-634-5100)

OAKDALE: site of the U.S. Immigration Department's Federal Detention Center. (Not open to the public.) Nearby, West Bay Wildlife Management Area is a 55,000-acre, heavily wooded tract off La. 10 and La. 26 for bird-watching, hunting, and bow hunting. Three state-maintained campsites are available. (318-491-2575)

OBERLIN: Allen Parish Courthouse, listed in the National Register of Historic Places, was completed in 1914. Two-story buff brick set on an English basement, it features classical baroque styling. **Allen Parish Fair** (early October).

KINDER: built with a western flavor and located on the Acadiana Trail. **The Kinder Area Arts Council** offers information on special exhibits, performances, and events. (318-738-5561). Fishing, camping, canoeing in nearby Calcasieu River and Bayou Serpent; Sauce Piquante and Music Festival held Labor Day weekend—food, dancing, entertainment.

ELTON: the Coushatta Indians moved here from settlements on the Tennessee River, bringing with them traditional skills such as basketry. The **Coushatta Indian Culture Center and Trading Post** exhibits artifacts of the tribe and sells pine needle baskets and other handcrafts. Open Mon.-Sat., 9-5. (318-584-2653). **Little Brick Outside Jail,** built in 1927 and located in the center of town, measures 14′ by 14′, has two compartments, two steel doors, and two windows.

JENNINGS: just north of Jennings is the Louisiana Oil and Gas Park (La. 26 at I-10), featuring a wooden replica of the first Louisiana oil well drilling rig (1901), nonworking displays of modern drilling equipment, Cajun houses, an Acadian Museum of historic items from early oil days, a large lake with recreation area, and a visitors center. Open daily. **The Jeff Davis Arts Council** offers information on special exhibits, performances, and events. (318-824-6593). **The Zigler Museum,** 411 Clara, presents a permanent collection of European, Asian, and American paintings, dioramas of Louisiana wildlife scenes, waterfowl woodcarvings, as well as changing exhibits. Open Tues.-Sat., 9-5; weekends, 2-5. Free. (318-824-0114). **Jennings Carnegie Public Library,** 303 Gary, is a Palladian-style building with octagonal rotunda funded by Andrew Carnegie in 1908. Houses extensive genealogical library. (318-821-5517). **W. H. Tupper General Store Museum,** 311 N. Main, features exhibits of a turn-of-the-century general store as well as Indian baskets. Admission. (318-821-5531). Tour of homes second Sunday in December. Admission. (318-824-0114). Scenic drive—La. 26 through the Cajun prairie from Jennings to Lake Arthur.

LAKE ARTHUR: the lake and surrounding area offer excellent recreational opportunities for sailing, fishing, and hunting.

LACASSINE NATIONAL WILDLIFE REFUGE: over 31,000 acres of natural preserve marshland for ducks, geese and other waterfowl, and small animals. Open March through October.

LAKE CHARLES: Southwest Louisiana's largest city, incorporated in 1867, was once a haven for pirates, including the legendary Jean Lafitte, who are reputed to have hidden their contraband in the intricate network of backwaters and bayous. The city is named for Charles Sallier, one of the first French settlers who arrived in the 1760s. Lake Charles is a petrochemical and industrial city and the state's third largest port, connected by a 40-mile manmade ship channel to the Gulf of Mexico. Recreational opportunities abound on the area lakes, bayous, and rivers. Deep-sea fishing in the Gulf is nearby.

Southwest Louisiana Convention and Visitors Bureau, 1211 N. Lakeshore. Tourist information and brochures. Open weekdays, 8-5. (800-456-SWLA). **The Calcasieu Arts and Humanities Council** offers information on special exhibits, performances, and events. (318-433-3921 or 436-7483). **Imperial Calcasieu Museum,** Ethel at Sallier streets. The museum contains original Audubon prints, historical exhibits, artifacts and records of Lake Charles, and changing art exhibits. The 300-year-old Sallier oak is in the museum's back yard. Tues.-Fri., 10-5; weekends, 1-5. Admission. (318-439-3797). **North Beach** is a manmade white sand beach on the shore of Lake Charles; LaFleur Beach is south of town off I-210. Admission in season. **The Historic Charpentier District** is an architecturally unique area of Victorian homes with distinctive ornamentation, now described as Lake Charles-style architecture, comprising approximately 20 square blocks. Walking or riding tours with an explanatory brochure. **Children's Museum**, 809 Kirby Street, features hands-on exhibits and participatory programs for children 3-14. Tues.-Fri., 10-5; Sat., 10-4; Sun., 2-5. Admission. (318-433-9421). **Bilbo Cemetery,** located on the Lake Charles waterfront on land that was once the site of the Cantonment Atkinson, a military housing structure established in 1829. **McNeese State University** library displays a collection of Federal duck prints. For information on other special exhibits and performances at McNeese, call (318-477-2520). **Contraband Days** is a 12-day festival beginning with "Jean Lafitte the pirate's invasion" of Lake Charles and features pageants, boat races, parades, contests, music, and entertainment. Late April-early May.

   SAM HOUSTON JONES STATE PARK, La. 378, 12 miles north of Lake Charles, at the intersection of the Houston River, west fork of the Calcasieu, and Indian Bayou. Boating, cabins, camping, fishing, and nature trails are offered in the 1,068-acre park. Fees. (318-855-2665)

   DEQUINCY: originally settled in 1895 at the junction of two major railroads. **DeQuincy Railroad Museum,** 218 Lake Charles Avenue, housed in a restored turn-of-the-century depot, contains local historic memorabilia, railroading artifacts, and several restored rail cars. Open weekdays, 9-5. Free. (318-786-2823). **The country-Gothic All Saints Episcopal Church** is listed on the National Register.

   SULPHUR: established in 1913, 8 years after the beginning of sulphur mining at the nearby sulphur dome, discovered in 1865 by oil prospectors. The Brimstone Museum, 800 Picard Road, offers exhibits pertaining to southwest Louisiana, and especially the process of extracting sulphur as developed by German scientist Herman Frasch. Open weekdays, 9:30-5. Tourist information. (318-527-7142). Located in Frasch Park, with an 18-hole golf course. The Calcasieu-Cameron Free Fair offers agricultural and crafts exhibits, carnival, fireworks, and entertainment. First week in October. A Christmas Parade is a mid-December tradition.

CREOLE NATURE TRAIL is a driving tour that begins in Sulphur and follows Louisiana highways 27, 82 (called Hug the Coast Highway), 384, and 385 to explore the marshlands and Gulf Coast, returning to Lake Charles. **The Intracoastal Waterway** is a 1,116-mile channel, 125 feet wide and 12 feet deep, serving primarily barge traffic across the entire Gulf Coast from Brownsville, Texas to south of Tallahassee, Florida. **Hackberry** on La. 27, named for an indigenous tree, is called the crab capital of the world. Processing plants prepare crab for commercial markets. Marsh tours, hunting, and fishing available. **The Sabine National Wildlife Refuge,** comprised of over 140,000 acres of brackish and freshwater marsh, is part of the Mississippi and Central Flyways and home to numerous species of wildlife—alligators, red wolf, and falcon among them. Sabine Refuge headquarters, open Mon.-Fri., 7-4, weekends, 12-4, offers information about the refuge and well-designed exhibits of wildlife, ecology, and habitats. (318-762-3816). The Marsh Trail is a 1-mile walking trail through the marsh to an observation tower providing anover view of the habitat. Alligators, birds, and small animals are often seen at close range. Insect repellent is suggested for mosquito protection.

Holly Beach, on a 26-mile stretch of beach, is popular for swimming, shelling, camping, fishing, and bird-watching. Offshore oil platforms, visible from the beach, were first introduced in 1946. To the west is **Johnson's Bayou,** home of the Holleyman Bird Sanctuary, a coastal chenier where migratory songbirds rest and feed. Not developed—use boots and insect repellent. **Calcasieu River** and the deep-water ship channel separate the Louisiana Gulf strip; crossings on a car ferry that operates 24 hours. **Cameron,** a center for seafood and oil industries, is home to the **Fur and Wildlife Festival** (second weekend in January) and the Deep Sea Fishing Rodeo (July 4 weekend). Our Lady Star of the Sea Monument, on La. 82, is a statue erected to invoke protection from hurricanes. Leesburg Museum, Henry Street off La. 82, depicts the area's history. Inquire about hours. **Rutherford Beach,** south of La. 82, is popular for surf fishing and swimming. **The Cheniers** (pronounced shuh-neer) are unusual formations of sand and shell ridges, formerly beaches, on which moss-draped oaks grow, a peculiar and scenic phenomenon in the marsh. Oak Grove is named for the clusters of ancient live oaks that line the highways along the cheniers. Slightly to the north are Little Chenier and Chenier Perdu, where wild iris meadows bloom in the spring and remnants of an Attakapas Indian village can sometimes be found. **The**

Rockefeller Wildlife Refuge, a 50-mile roundtrip east from Oak Grove, is 84,000 acres of protected marsh in Cameron and Vermilion parishes. A winter home for waterfowl and year-round preserve for wildlife, Rockefeller is open to visitors March 1 through Nov. 30 for sightseeing and sport fishing (permit required). Animals on display all year near refuge headquarters. (318-538-2165). Also, artifacts from *El Nuevo Constante,* an 18th-century Spanish merchant ship wrecked off this coast and discovered in 1979, are on display at the refuge offices. **Cameron Prairie National Wildlife Refuge**, La. 27 between Creole and Lake Charles, is a 9,600-acre preserve for wintering waterfowl and wildlife. Public boat launch available. Open weekdays, 8-4:30. (318-598-2216).

VINTON: is located in the old Rio Hondo territory, a no-man's land disputed by Spain and the United States. **Delta Downs Racetrack,** La. 3063, has quarterhorse and thoroughbred races. Admission; no minors. (318-389-7441). **Old Lyons Home,** 1335 Horridge Street, on the National Register, was built of pine and cypress in 1900; the brick carriage house was added in 1916. The home is elaborate Queen Anne style with Eastlake ornamentation and was one of the first houses west of the Calcasieu River to have electricity. By appt. (318-589-2903)

I-10 EASTBOUND LOUISIANA TOURIST INFORMATION CENTER near the Texas border has a raised walkway through a natural swamp setting and picnic area, restrooms. Information and brochures. (318-589-7774)

OLD SPANISH TRAIL: originally a Spanish trading route, crosses west Calcasieu from the I-10 Eastbound Louisiana Tourist Information Center near the Texas border to Sulphur. Much of U.S. 90 is built on the original path, which linked Texas and New Orleans. **Niblett's Bluff,** west of Vinton on La. 109, was a busy river port before the Civil War and offered safe passage for crossing the Sabine River. Confederate breastworks remain in the park, which offers boat launch and camping. A bike trail offers scenery to walkers and bikers. Open daily, 6 A.M.-10 P.M. Fees. **Sabine Island Wildlife Management Area** can be approached on Niblett's Bluff Road west off La. 109. This 8,100-acre tract located between the Sabine River and Old River and Big Bayou offers hunting, trapping, excellent fishing, boating, and waterskiing. No camping. (318-491-2575). **Vinton** (see above). **Antioch Baptist Church** and Big Woods Cemetery near Edgerly, established in 1827 and restored in 1974, was one of the first area churches.

Unique Louisiana

CREOLE NATURE TRAIL

In the low, flat reaches of Cameron Parish marshland, where a bridge over the Intracoastal Canal looms like an erector-set castle, where, at certain angles, the sky domes 180 degrees, lies a loop of roadways called the Creole Nature Trail. Winding across the heel of the Louisiana boot, it cuts through a vast territory that appears as a vacant wasteland but is, instead, a unique and precious environment.

South from Sulphur, the flat farmland becomes marshland, a far-reaching, almost treeless expanse of grass and reeds cut through with meandering slow-water streams and placid lakes. Civilization erupts at Hackberry, "Crab Capital of the World" it calls itself, where a webwork of masts and lines denote the huddle of fishing fleets awaiting favorable tides.

Standard, yellow road signs along the no-shouldered highway offer surprises, such as the black silhouette of an alligator—a wordless reminder that this is the natural habitat of a certain fearsome reptile; keep your eyes open.

In the channels near the road, stick-legged water birds pose statuary-still. Regiments of ducks and geese flock-float overhead and songbirds flutter about the black electrical wires like kinetic notes on an interminable staff. Occasionally, deer and small game bound into view.

At the Sabine National Wildlife Reserve headquarters, an introduction to the complex ecology and inhabitants of the marsh is presented in a thoughtful and easy-to-understand exhibit, an explicative teaser to the excitement of actually following the well-marked, mile-long marsh walking trail. The alligators near the trail in a somnolent state could be stuffed, Disneyworld effects until they jerk reality with a quick and deliberate snap of their jaws, or slide soundlessly into the water, scaly mud-colored head easing just above the waterline.

Between the marsh and the fierce and infinite Gulf of Mexico is a brown sand stripe from Holly Beach to Johnson's Bayou that locals reverentially call "The Cajun Riviera." It's a gritty beach, a jumble of shells, driftwood, and the flotsam of life offshore—debris from boats and the pinnacle oil rigs easily seen in the distance. Along the beach, a casual line of shacks and cabins, souvenir and fishing shops, and fast-food purveyors face the Gulf, outposts of Cajun hospitality, sentinels for the terror of hurricanes.

A ferry scuttles highway traffic across the well-travelled, deepwater channel at Calcasieu Pass to Cameron, home of the rugged January Fur and Wildlife Festival, a plethora of oil industry services, and the venerated fish processing plants, whose emanations make the plants' presence known when the wind blows from anywhere but north.

East of Cameron, the cheniers emerge eerily from the marshland. (Though the word chenier means "cluster of oak trees" in French, in south Louisiana, it is pronounced *"sha-neer."*) On relic beaches and sandbars, left behind when the Gulf ebbed, massive oaks and other unlikely vegetation have taken hold, creating dark green, mysterious island outcroppings in the otherwise flat, emerald marsh. The oaks and bald cypress, bent and twisted by Gulf winds, form a ruff along the edges of the cheniers, which flutter and chirrup during migration seasons, alive with thick communities of birdlife.

The Rockefeller Wildlife Refuge at Grand Chenier, though open all year as a research station, welcomes visitors from March through September to sightsee and fish with a permit. The intrepid can hike the manmade dike two miles out into the marsh, pioneering through the overgrowth to revel at the sights of roseate spoonbills gliding past like raspberry splashes, the bomber-breasted pelicans careening toward unseen fish, and a variety of other fascinating migratory waterfowl. Past dike's end and a short swathe of sloggy, floating marsh, the brown sand, scalloped with foam and shell lace, stretches undisturbed as far as the eye can see.

A day exploring the Creole Nature Trail creates not only a lasting memory but, perhaps more importantly, the stunning realization that a wasteland is merely a place defined by people who look with uninformed eyes.

Wildlife in the marshes along the Creole Nature Trail. (Courtesy Louisiana Office of Tourism)

Lafayette Area

5

Lafayette
and Acadiana

Acadiana—land of the Acadiennes, or Cajuns—is the area where the Nova Scotian French emigrants settled in the mid-18th century after being expelled from Canada. Primarily French-speaking farmers, they arrived and settled along bayous and on the prairie. Over the years, traces of Spanish, German, English, African, and Indian mores filtered into their culture, influencing it. As a result, the Cajun culture is now regarded as unique in the United States. The language, food, music, and traditions have become widely known, and elements of the Cajun lifestyle have been popularized to the point of commercialization. It is ironic, perhaps, because several decades ago the Cajun culture was threatened with total acculturation and loss of identity. Evangeline, St. Landry, Acadia, Vermilion, Lafayette, Iberia, St. Martin, and St. Mary are the parishes comprising this area, with the city of Lafayette as the largest metropolitan center.

COCODRIE LAKE: between Rapides and Evangeline parishes, once the site of an Indian village which was flooded, according to legend. A cypress-studded cover offers good fishing. Boat rentals.

CROOKED CREEK RECREATION AREA: La. 3187 off La. 13, offers a manmade beach on Crooked Creek Reservoir, with fishing, swimming, boating, sailing, picnicking, camping. (318-599-2661)

BAYOU CHICOT: La. 167 at 106, probably the oldest settlement in Evangeline Parish and the original site of the two oldest Protestant congregations west of the Mississippi River. Calvary Baptist Church, organized in 1812, was built in the early 1900s, and the United Methodist Church, organized in 1807, was built in 1907. **The Ferguson Cemetery** contains graves dating to the early 19th century.

CHICOT STATE PARK: located 6 miles north of Ville Platte on La.

3042 offers dense woodlands surrounding a 2,000-acre lake stocked for fishing. A 6,500-acre park offers swimming, trails, picnicking, boating, camping, cabins. Fees. (318-363-2403)

LOUISIANA STATE ARBORETUM: 2 miles north of Chicot State Park is a 600-acre preserve of rolling hills and nature trails where over 100 species of labeled Louisiana native and southern plants can be found. **The Caroline Dormon Lodge** houses a library and herbarium. Interpretive program and tours available. Open Wed.-Sun., 9-5. Gardens open daily. (318-363-2503)

CAZAN'S LAKE: located on La. 29 east of Chicot, a 1,000-acre park offering camping, cabins, as well as a 900-acre lake for fishing and 600-acre lake specifically developed for crawfishing. Boat rentals. Fees. (318-363-1558)

MILLER'S LAKE: La. 376, one of Louisiana's best bass lakes offers fishing, boating, boat rentals.

VILLE PLATTE: its name means "flat city" in French, possibly derived from its location, where the hills of Bayou Chicot meet the flat Gulf Coastal Plain. The town was founded by Maj. Marcellin Garand, a soldier of France who served with Napoleon, and was on the Old Spanish Trail. Marcellin's grave may be seen in the Old Town Cemetery. **Ville Platte Chamber of Commerce** offers tourist information, maps, and brochures for Evangeline Parish. (318-363-1878). **Evangeline Arts Association** offers information on special exhibits, performances, and events. (318-363-7110). **The Louisiana Cotton Festival,** held the second weekend in October, has parades and a fais-do-do, and climaxes on Sunday with the **Tournoi de las Ville Platte,** which dates back locally over a century. The turnoi is a form of medieval jousting in which costumed riders on horseback thrust lances through small iron rings. **Mardi Gras,** including entertainment in the street and a Courir de Mardi Gras, the country horseback run, is held on Fat Tuesday. Several private residences exemplify Acadian architecture and are worth a drive-by: **O.E. Guillory House,** built in 1835, is one of the oldest in town and is partially restored. **Louis DeVille House,** of cypress with a split-shingle roof, is just off the junction of La. 167 and 10. **Johnson Place,** built with bousillage walls, is in disrepair. **Octave Thompson House,** built in 1914, incorporates some materials of an earlier dwelling on this site and is in the style of the early settlers' cottages. **Aldes Vidrine House,** La. 363 east, is an early French settler plantation house with outside stairway and a long gallery with adobe façade.

MAMOU: site of one of the most colorful and well-known Mardi Gras courirs, held on Fat Tuesday. At **Fred's Bar,** 420 6th, live Cajun radio broadcast from 8 to 11 A.M. every Saturday. Admission. **Cajun Music and Fall Festival** presents a battle of the Cajun bands, boucherie, and entertainment.

THISTLEWAITE WILDLIFE MANAGEMENT AREA: near Beggs, on La. 10. 11,000-acre tract of bottomland hardwood offers hunting, trapping by permit. All-weather roads. No camping. (318-942-7553)

BEGGS: Homeplace, built in 1826, is a 1 1/2-story cypress house built on a Spanish land grant and furnished with antiques and historic artifacts. Drive-by.

WASHINGTON: this small town is one of Louisiana's oldest settlements, dating from 1822, and was once an important center of commerce because of its location on navigable Bayou Cortableau. The last steamboat called in 1900, and the town still retains much of its 19th-century character and charm. Part of it is a National Register Historic District. **Historic Washington Museum and Tourist Information Center,** corner of Main and DeJean in the old Town Hall, offers information, maps, and brochures for walking or riding tours. Open 10-5. (318-826-3626). **Starvation Point,** built in the 1790s at the confluence of bayous Boeuf and Cocodrie, is a 2-story brick antebellum home originally used as a trading post and overnight stop for travellers. Drive-by. **Nicholson House of History,** 303 Main, built in 1835, features a fort below the front porch with portholes for firing rifles and an upstairs Confederate hospital room. By appt. (318-826-3670). **De la Morandiere,** 515 St. John, built in 1830, is a 2-story French planter's cypress cottage. By appt. (318-826-3626). **Hinckley Home,** 405 De-Jean, a late-18th-century house, contains steamboat memorabilia and heirloom antiques, with a family cemetery dating to 1803. By appt. (318-826-3906). **Arlington Plantation,** La. 103, built in 1829, is a 3-story brick house with a cellar and a long double gallery overlooking the bayou. Drive-by.

Magnolia Ridge, La. 103, completed in 1830 in Greek Revival style, contains antiques and served as headquarters for both Union and Confederate troops. Grounds open; house private. **Camellia Cove,** built in 1825, is restored and furnished with heirlooms and maintains its original separate kitchen. By appt. (318-826-7362). **Old Washington Cemetery,** Vine, contains graves dating to early 1800s, including victims of the 1850s yellow fever epidemic. **Hebrew Rest Cemetery,** Vine, is a Jewish cemetery dating from the early 1800s. **Lastrapes Oak,** La. 10 south, is a member of the Live Oak Society and consists of 7 intertwining trunks, supposedly planted by Jean Lastrapes for his 7 sons and never transplanted. Private, can be seen from the road.

Festival de Courtableu features tour of homes and historic buildings, arts and crafts, music. Third weekend in March.

KROTZ SPRINGS: an oil wildcatter, Al Krotz, discovered artesian water here while looking for oil. Access to the west side of the Atchafalaya Basin from Krotz Springs offers fishing, boating, hunting, and camping.

PORT BARRE: called "birthplace of the Teche," where it springs from Bayou Courtableau. Teche is the Indian word for "snake," and this bayou was immortalized by Longfellow's *Evangeline*. Birthplace-of-the-Teche Park is a triangle of land located where the bayou begins with a small Acadian museum housing local artifacts. Camping nearby. Information from City Hall. (318-585-7646)

OPELOUSAS: founded by the French in 1720 as a trading post for the Indians, Poste des Opelousas is on the Acadian Trail. It was made the seat of St. Landry Parish in 1805 and served as state capital during the Civil War. Tourist information, maps, and brochures available at **Opelousas-St. Landry Tourist Information,** 220 Academy (318-924-2683), or at the **Jim Bowie Museum and Tourist Information Center,** U.S. 190 east. **Le Vieux Village,** 220 Academy, is a collection of vintage structures depicting historic St. Landry. **Jim Bowie Museum** contains a collection of Bowie memorabilia from the time he lived in Opelousas. Open daily, 8-4. (318-948-6263). **Michel Prudhomme Home,** early 19th century, a beautiful French Colonial home owned by the man who donated land in 1797 to St. Landry Church for a building site. By appt. (318-942-9602). **Mt. Olive Baptist Church,** founded in 1897 as the Black Academy at Mt. Olive Baptist Church. **Estorge Home,** 427 N. Market, built in 1827, is in the neoclassical style. Drive-by. **The Old Ray Homestead,** 378 Bellevue, built in 1853, was used during the Civil War as a Confederate Medical Department headquarters. By appt. (318-948-6784). **Governor's Mansion,** W. Grolee at Bellevue, built in 1848, was the governor's mansion when Opelousas was the acting state capital. Drive-by. Brick sidewalks still remain from the early 19th century on many Opelousas streets. A large section laid in 1838 still remains on E. Grolee. **Lou Ana Foods,** N. Railroad, offers tours of the vegetable oil processing plant. By appt. (318-948-6561). **Creole Foods,** Lombard St., offers tours of Tony Chachere's Creole Seasoning processing. By appt. (318-948-6784). **Louisiana Yambilee Festival,** held the last weekend in October, celebrates the Louisiana sweet potato with exhibits, food, livestock show, entertainment, parade. (318-948-8848). **Cajun Christmas,** second weekend in December, features a parade and a wagon tour of old Opelousas, as well as other activities. (318-948-6784). **International Cajun Joke Tellers**

Contest is held the third weekend in April and features the art of Cajun joke- and storytelling. **Zydeco Festival,** near Plaisance, Parish Road 5753 off U.S. 167, is held on the Saturday before Labor Day, noon to dark. Zydeco music, food, arts and crafts. Admission. (318-942-2392)

LAWTELL: U.S. 190, Matt's Museum exhibits old newspapers, early documents (many hand-written), steamboat vouchers, Civil War memorabilia, and Acadian artifacts. Open. Admission.

EUNICE: an auction of lots held at the Midland Branch Railroad Depot in 1894 created the city named for the wife of C. C. Duson. Tourist information, maps, and brochures available from the **Tourist Information Center,** City Hall (318-457-7389). **Eunice Museum,** housed in the Midland Branch Railroad Depot, exhibits auction records, historic Cajun memorabilia, and artifacts. Tues.-Sat., 9-12, 1-5. (318-457-6540) **Liberty Theatre,** Second at Park, a grand 1920s-vintage theatre, has been restored. Live Cajun radio broadcasts, featuring vaudeville-type live entertainment (French-speaking) every Saturday evening, 6-8 P.M. Admission. **Jean Lafitte National Historic Park-Acadian Culture Center** features interpretative programs and exhibits showcasing Acadian culture, including archives, crafts, folk medicine, foods, and heritage. Open daily, 9-5. (318-264-6862). **LSU-Eunice,** a branch of the state university system, located south of Eunice, schedules some special events. (318-457-7311). **Mardi Gras,** a 4-day celebration before and on Fat Tuesday, including a Cajun ball, entertainment, and traditional Courir de Mardi Gras. **World Championship Crawfish Etouffée Cook-off,** last Sunday in March, focuses on one of the area's most significant agricultural products. Costumed teams in cooking contest, music, dancing.

BASILE: La. 371, north of U.S. 190, incorporated in 1911 after the area had been settled in the early 1800s by pioneers, lumbermen, and ranchers. **Cajun Mardi Gras** celebrated on Fat Tuesday includes a Courir de Mardi Gras, community gumbo, and street dancing. **Louisiana Swine Festival,** held the first weekend in November, features hog-calling, street parade, greasy pig contest, boucherie, barn dancing, and music. **Eunice Arts Festival,** City Hall and Park Avenue grounds, held the second Sunday in May, features bands, storytellers, puppet show, food, arts and crafts exhibits, and demonstrations.

CHURCH POINT: La. 95, the traditional Courir de Mardi Gras takes place the Sunday before Mardi Gras and includes the masked riders, community gumbo, street dancing. **The Buggy Festival,** held July 4 weekend, seeks to recreate old times with a buggy and covered-wagon parade, accordion and fiddle contests, food.

BRANCH: La. 35, the site of the **Heritage Farm Village,** an expansive farm complex that includes a Cajun house built in 1852 and a museum of pioneer farm life in the bayou country. Open Mon.-Sat., ll-5; Sun., 9-6. Admission. (318-334-2949). **Acadiana Fish Farm,** La. 365, offers fishing. Bring your own containers. Fish will be cleaned for you. Fees.

SUNSET: Chretien Point Plantation, located off La. 93 about 4 miles south of Sunset, is Louisiana's oldest original Greek Revival plantation house, built in 1831 and fully restored to elegance after a period of disrepair. Open daily except holidays, 10-5. Admission. (318-233-7050)

LEONVILLE: built by free men of color, some of whose descendants still live here, now a yam shipping center. Some Acadian and German pioneer homes along the Teche still remain.

GRAND COTEAU: some of the oldest and finest oak and pine alleys are located at historic Academy of the Sacred Heart, built in 1821, and St. Charles College, built in 1818, where 19th-century Creole bluebloods received their education. Many antebellum houses and structures are found in the town, designated as a National Register Historic District, but are private. Drive-by. **The Academy of the Sacred Heart** quartered Federal troops during the Civil War and is still a Catholic girls' school. The main building, circa 1831, is surrounded by oaks and formal gardens. The shrine of St. John Berchmans is erected on the only site in the United States where in 1866 a miracle is said to have occurred. For information on tours call 318-662-5275. **The St. Charles Borromeo Catholic Church,** completed in 1880, is one of the oldest wooden churches in the country and features paintings by Erasmus Humbrecht, three sets of beautiful stained-glass windows, and a unique bell tower. Tours by appt. Admission. (318-662-5279 or 662-3875). **St. Charles Borromeo Cemetery,** behind the church, is a tree-shaded, picturesque site with graves dating to the early 19th century. **Festival of Grand Coteau,** held in December on the grounds of St. Charles Church and College, celebrates the town's heritage with tours, entertainment, buggy rides, and food.

HENDERSON: La. 347 off I-10, is one of the prime entry points from the west to the Atchafalaya Basin. Boat rentals, guides. Guided tours of the swamp—admission.

ATCHAFALAYA BASIN: the nation's largest river basin swamp is a unique complex of habitats extending over 800,000 acres, including hardwood forests, cypress swamps, marshes, and bayous. Considered one of the best wilderness areas and a prime area for fishing, crawfishing, hunting, and trapping, as well some farming and rich oil and gas fields, it is also part of the Mississippi River control system, funneling the overflow of the Red and Mississippi rivers to the Gulf of Mexico. Many people live in the Basin, but Butte La Rose, off I-10, is one of the few settlements that exist between the levees of the floodway. La. 96 east of Catahoula provides an excellent view of the Atchafalaya Basin's majesty.

BREAUX BRIDGE: La. 31, bills itself as the "crawfish capital of the world," and is the site of the annual **Crawfish Festival,** the first weekend in May, featuring crawfish eating contest, music, bayou parade, crawfish races. **Arnaud Robert Oak,** a member of the Live Oak Society, is the second largest oak in the state.

LAFAYETTE: Lafayette Parish was formed from St. Martin Parish in 1823 and reached to the Gulf of Mexico until 1844 when Vermilion Parish was carved out of its southern reaches. Jean Mouton laid out the town in 1824, calling it Vermilionville, and it became the parish seat. In the 1830s, steamboats came up the Vermilion River but were limited by its narrow width. Its most important growth began when the railroad came in 1880 and again, in 1952, with the development of the Oil Center. **The Lafayette Parish Convention and Visitors Bureau,** near the intersection of I-10 and I-49, offers information, maps, and brochures of the area. Open weekdays, 8:30-5; weekends, 9-5. (318-232-3808 or 800-346-1958, U.S., and 800-543-5340, Canada). **Acadiana Arts Council** offers information on special exhibits, performances, and events. (318-233-7060). **Lafayette Museum,** 1122 Lafayette, once the Maison Dimanche, or Sunday home, of Louisiana's first Democratic governor, Alexandre Mouton, exhibits heirlooms of the Mouton family, antiques, memorabilia, and artifacts of local culture. Special Christmas exhibits during the Victorian Christmas display. Open Tues.-Sat., 9-5; Sun., 3-5. Admission. (318-234-2208). **Old City Hall,** 217 Main, first occupied in 1889, is noted for its Victorian architecture with Romanesque influence. **Lafayette Art Gallery**, 700 Lee Avenue, features exhibits by local and regional artists. Open Tues.-Fri., 10-4; Sat., 10-2. (318-269-0363)

Lafayette Natural History Museum and Planetarium, 6371 Girard Park Drive, features changing special exhibits dedicated to a wide range of environmental studies. Workshops, films, and special programs. Open Mon., Wed.-Fri., 9-5; Tues., 9-9; weekends, 1-5. Donation. Planetarium shows on diverse subjects scheduled Tuesday evenings and Sunday afternoons. (318-268-5544). **Acadiana Park Nature Station and Trail,** a facility of the Natural History Museum located in Acadiana Park on Alexander Street, offers an interpretive program through the visitors' center and a well-marked nature trail through the bottomland hardwood preserve. Open weekdays, 9-5; weekends,

1-5. Camping with hookups. (318-261-8348). **Heymann Oil Center,** around Heymann Boulevard, founded by the late Maurice Heymann in 1952, a 1-story office park for oil and oil-related companies, a very original concept at the time. **St. John's Cathedral,** 914 St. John, built in 1918 in German Romanesque style, containing a bishop's chair. Built on the site of Jean Mouton's original chapel. St. John's Oak, estimated to be 400 years old, grows in the cathedral yard. **Mouton Home,** 338 N. Sterling, built in 1848, with the lower floor of bousillage and the upper floors of pegged cypress, served as headquarters of Union general Nathaniel Banks during the Civil War. Drive-by.

University of Southwestern Louisiana, University at Johnston, is one of the state's largest public universities. *Cypress Lake* in the center of the campus is a natural swamp with native iris, cypress trees, swamp plants, and alligators. *Ira Nelson Horticulture Center* includes a tropical botanical garden, orchid garden, and experimental flower garden. *French House,* now used as a language lab, contains a collection of furniture constructed by Henri Bendel. (By appt., 318-233-3850.) *University Art Museum,* 101 Girard Park Drive, has a permanent collection of 19th-and 20th-century art, silver, and glass, and offers special exhibits of both contemporary and historical art, photography, and related media. Permanent collection open Mon.-Fri., 9-4. Fletcher Hall, E. Lewis at Girard Park Drive, open Mon.-Fri., 9-4; Sun., 2-5. (318-231-5326). For information on special campus exhibits, performances, or events, call (318-231-6000 or 231-6940). **Hebrew Cemetery,** Lee at University, contains a bronze monument imported by Henri Bendel in memory of his mother, featuring a mourning figure and an angel pointing toward heaven. **Girard Park,** site of a Civil War battle, has picnic facilities, swimming pool, tennis courts, and other recreation.

Acadian Village off Ridge Road south of La. 342, a relocated and restored Acadian community from the early 1800s, is comprised of furnished chapel, general store, several authentic period homes, and Missionary Museum, as well as a folk museum with artifacts. Open daily except holidays, 10-5. Admission. Special Christmas light display, late November-second weekend of December. Admission. (318-981-2364). **Vermilionville,** Surrey Street, is a Cajun-Creole living history and folklife museum set on the banks of Bayou Vermilion depicting life in the area from 1765 to 1890. Many vernacular buildings, working craftsmen, music, cooking demonstrations, and special events. Open daily, 9-5, except Christmas and New Year's Day. Admission. (318-233-0477 or 800-992-2968). A number of Lafayette's historic homes and buildings are private, or have been adaptively renovated. Ask tourist information for locations. **Bayou Belle Riverboat** plies the

Vermilion River from Vermilionville to Pinhook Landing (Pinhook Road). Schedule available. Admission. **Azalea Trail,** spectacular marked floral trail to drive in mid-March or whenever the azaleas bloom.

Festivals Acadiens, encompassing several festivals at once, takes place the third weekend in September. Cajun food, music, crafts and skills, and folklife are featured, as are arts. Located in front of the Museum of Natural History, in Girard Park, and other locations. Some events free, others charge admission. (318-232-3808). **Festival International de Louisiane,** third weekend in April, takes place in downtown Lafayette and consists of food, music, performing arts, folk arts, and special children's programs, presented by French-speaking cultures from around the world. (318-232-8086). **Mardi Gras** here is the second largest Fat Tuesday celebration in Louisiana, beginning on Twelfth Night with large krewe balls, culminating on the Monday before Mardi Gras with the Queen's and Children's Parade. It is followed on Tuesday by a costume contest at 9 A.M., parades with floats, throws, and marching bands, and an afternoon parade open to anyone who wants to participate. The annual Southwest Louisiana Mardi Gras Association Pageant and Ball is held at the Heymann Performing Arts Center in the evening, open to the public. Free with ticket. (318-233-2705)

CARENCRO: La. 182, was originally part of the Beau Bassin area settled by the Acadians. In 1874, Saint Pierre—Saint Peter—the first church in the area, was established and the area named for the church where old French family names are still carved in the pews. When the railroad came, the name reverted to Carencro. **Evangeline Downs,** La. 167 north, features thoroughbred racing April through Labor Day. Parimutuel betting. No minors. Admission. (318-896-6185). **St. Peter's Catholic Church,** 102 Church Street, was built in 1904. Open daily. Tours by appt. (318-8910)

RAYNE: calls itself the "Frog Capital of the World," and is the center of Louisiana's frog industry, one of the nation's largest commercial shippers of frogs. The annual **Frog Festival,** held the second weekend in September, features frog-racing and jumping contests, a fais-do-do, food (including frogs' legs). (318-334-2332)

CROWLEY: founded in 1887 and became the parish seat the same year. The rapid turn-of-the-century growth of the community was due to the rice industry. A National Register Historic District with an impressive area of fine Victorian homes and a courthouse square. **The Greater Crowley Chamber of Commerce,** N. Parkerson, offers tourist information, maps, and brochures. (318-783-2108). **Rice Mill Row,**

was once the largest concentration of rice mills in the United States. **Rice Museum,** U.S. 90 west, features exhibits on Acadian culture, Crowley history, and the rice and oil industry, including replicas of a rice mill and machinery and tools. March-November, Wed.-Fri., 10-3 or by appt. Admission. (318-783-6842). **Blue Rose Museum,** Primeaux Road, west of La. 13, is an Acadian cottage built in 1848 and named for a variety of rice. The museum, moved from Youngsville, exhibits cut glass, crystal, china, silver, and Victoriana. By appt. Admission. (318-783-3096). **Wright Andrus House,** Lake Drive, a raised cottage with bousillage walls built in 1839, is furnished with excellent antiques. By appt. (318-783-3051). **International Rice Festival,** held in October, features a parade, livestock show, street fair, ball, and rice-eating contests.

ROBERTS COVE: La. 98, northeast of Crowley. This small community of German descendants welcomes St. Nicholas on December 15. **St. Leo's Church and cemetery** have German inscriptions.

GUEYDAN: founded in 1898, is a rice center and known for fishing and duck hunting. Guides available. **Old Peter's Church** was built in the mission style. **Gueydan Duck Festival** held Labor Day weekend features duck-and-goose-calling contests, skeet and turkey shoots, arts and crafts, dancing, parade, food. (318-536-6330)

KAPLAN: La. 35 at La. 14, a rice community with rice mills along the railroad. **The Acadian-style Maison de Memoires** contains furnishings of the period. By appt. (318-643-7478). **Bastille Day Celebration,** on the weekend closest to July 14, celebrates French freedom with games, rides, races, fireworks, and fais-do-do.

HUG THE COAST HIGHWAY: La. 82, is a great attraction for nature enthusiasts and bird-watchers; especially interesting are spring wildflowers, such as iris and water hyacinths, and migrating birds and waterfowl. The highway continues past the Rockefeller Wildlife Refuge. (For continuation, refer to Chapter 4, Lake Charles and the Southwest.)

PECAN ISLAND: on La. 82, is a chenier, one of the "oak islands" on remnant sandbars found in the marsh. Excellent duck hunting, with guides available and several private boat launches with fees.

MARSH ISLAND WILDLIFE REFUGE AND GAME PRESERVE: accessible by boat, this island between Vermilion Bay and the Gulf of Mexico is an 82,000-acre property, mainly flat, grassy marshland with lakes and bayous, considered one of the most important areas for migratory waterfowl and fur-bearing animals on the continent.

ABBEVILLE: the parish seat of Vermilion Parish was established in 1843 by Roman Catholic missionary Père Antoine Megret, a self-imposed exile from Vermilionville (Lafayette). It was laid out around two public squares. **Abbeville Tourist Information Center,** 1905 Veterans Memorial Drive, offers information, maps, brochures, and tours of the area. (318-893-2596). **Vermilion Arts Council** offers information on special exhibits, performances, and events. (318-893-2936). **St. Mary Magdalen Church,** built in 1910 in modified French Gothic style, is considered one of the most beautiful in Acadiana. A German baroque-style organ and beautiful finishing enhance the interior. **Magdalen Square,** one of the original two squares, is surrounded by a brick wall with a fountain in the center. **Vermilion Parish Courthouse** is a Greek Revival-style building located on the second town square. Paintings on the main floor hallway depict South Louisiana scenes. **Fairview Street,** which follows the curve of the river, offers a scenic drive and interesting turn-of-the-century homes. Drive-by. **Riviana Rice Mills,** Washington, is one of the largest rice milling complexes in the country. By appt. (318-893-2220). **Louisiana Cattle Festival and Fair,** held in October to honor dairymen, features parades, floats, street dancing, food, music, and contests. **French-Acadian Music Festival,** held the second Saturday after Easter, draws many local, often amateur, musicians. Held in the Comeaux Recreation Center in City Park.

ERATH: founded by late-19th-century Swiss immigrant August Erath, who built a railroad station in the style of a Swiss chalet. The town celebrates the Fourth of July with contests, including greased pole-climbing, food, and fais-do-do.

DELCAMBRE: known as the "Shrimp Capital of the World," it straddles Vermilion and Iberia parishes, with the colorful shrimp fleet docked on the Iberia side. Delcambre Canal (Bayou Carlin) links the town with the Gulf of Mexico. **Shrimp Boat Landing,** off La. 14, has covered picnic area, fishermen's wharf, shrimping supplies. **The Shrimp Festival,** in August, celebrates the native seafood with games, street fair, food, fais-do-do, and includes the blessing of the fleet on Sunday. Fishing guide services available for a fee.

JEFFERSON ISLAND: La. 14 and La. 675, **Live Oak Gardens** has recovered remarkably from a freak accident in which the salt dome under Lake Peigneur was accidently punctured, creating a giant whirlpool that dramatically affected the geography of the land. The gardens have been restored, with 20 acres of tropical foliage and immaculate landscaping with year-round blooms in the English garden style. Reception area with film. Gardens open daily, except Christmas and New Year's, 9-5. Admission. **Joseph Jefferson House,** built in 1870 by the famous actor, is unique in style, with varied architectural

influences and whimsies including a belvedere. Furnished to the period. Open daily, 9-6. Admission to gardens includes house and boat
tour on Lake Peigneur and Delcambre Canal. (318-365-3332)

AVERY ISLAND: La. 329. A hill rising uncharacteristically in the
flat salt marsh is likely to be the result of an underlying salt dome,
such as the one at **Avery Island.** J. M. Avery quarried rock salt here for
the Confederates; archeologists suggest prehistoric Indians knew of
the salt springs. The 200-acre **Jungle Gardens and bird sanctuary**
were developed by E. A. McIlhenny, offering walking and driving
paths, landscaped garden and natural areas, a variety of native plants
as well as introduced material, and a 1,000-year-old Buddha in a Chinese garden. **Bird City,** begun in 1893 with the establishment of an
egret colony, now contains a variety of water birds nesting on special,
piered structures. Open daily, 9-5; admission. (318-365-8173).
Tabasco Sauce factory tour features manufacturing and bottling pro-
cedure of the red pepper sauce. Open Mon.-Fri., 9-4; Sat., 9-12.

BROUSSARD: on La. 182, the town's main street, is a selection of
interesting Victorian houses constructed in archetypal style. **Louisiana
Boudin Festival,** the second weekend in February, features boudin
cooking and eating contests, arts and crafts, carnival rides, entertainment.

ST. MARTINVILLE: the banks of Bayou Teche are considered the
traditional site of the arrival of the Acadians in 1765, the year in which
the Poste des Attakapas became a military station. During the French
Revolution, a number of aristocrats settled in or near this community,
leading to its name, Le Petit Paris (the little Paris). **The St. Martinville
Tourist Commission** offers information, maps, and brochures (318-
988-5409). **Maison DuChamp,** Main at Evangeline, was completed in
1876 as a city house of a planter, who lived out of town, served as the
U.S. Post Office, and now houses the visitor reception center. The second floor is a museum, with period rooms and a picture gallery of St.
Martinville history. Open weekdays, 9-3. Admission. (318-394-2229)

The Evangeline Oak, Evangeline Boulevard at Bayou Teche, is the
legendary tree under which Evangeline, returning from her long
journey, discovers that Gabriel is betrothed to someone else. On the
grounds of the former Old Castillo Hotel, built about 1790. Admission. (318-394-4010). **Town Square** is location of *St. Martin de Tours
Church,* the mother church of the Acadians. The parish was established
in 1765, but the present structure dates from 1832, incorporating sections of the original building as well as box pews, baptismal font, and
altar. *Evangeline Monument,* on the right side behind the church, marks
the grave of Emmeline Labiche, heroine of Longfellow's poem, *Evan-*

Snowy egrets building nests in the wildlife sanctuary on Avery Island.
(Courtesy Louisiana Office of Tourism)

geline. Le Petit Paris Museum on the right side of the church, constructed in 1861 and used as a school, features local arts and crafts, church records and documents, and an exhibit of Mardi Gras costumes. Open Mon.-Sat., 9-4:30; Sun., 10-4:30. (318-394-7334). Admission. *The Presbytere,* or priest's house, built in 1856, has been restored and furnished with period antiques, some original. Open daily, 2-4. Admission. Guided tours of the landscaped square, the Presbytere, church, and monuments leave from the Museum. Admission.

St. Martin Parish Courthouse, E. Main, is a Greek Revival structure built in 1838, housing records dating from 1760. **St. Michael's Cemetery,** near the church, contains graves that date from the late 1700s, many inscribed in French with flowery phrases. **La Grande Boucherie des Cajuns,** held in City Park the Sunday before Mardi Gras, showcases Acadian butchery customs, arts and crafts, foods, entertainment. (318-394-4215). **Mardi Gras** is celebrated with a ball held the Saturday evening before Fat Tuesday in the National Guard Armory. Open to the public. Admission. **Pine and Oak Alley,** La. 96 east, is a section left from a 2-mile-long alley that extended to Bayou Teche. Legend holds that plantation owner Charles Durand, who planted the trees, released spiders among them to spin webs through them, on which he sprinkled gold and silver dust for his daughter's wedding. **Stations of the Cross,** La. 96 east to Catahoula, is celebrated on Good Friday when the priest from Catahoula leads his congregation (in cars) to pray at each station, posted on trees along the road. **Longfellow-Evangeline State Commemorative Area,** La. 31, along Bayou Teche, is a 157-acre facility commemorating not only the poem, but the history of the Acadians. The Acadian Crafts shop, housed in a Cajun cottage, displays unique crafts of the Acadian culture. **Acadian House Museum,** built in 1765, exhibits original construction techniques— bousillage walls, handmade bricks, pegged cypress—and period furniture. The smokehouse, kitchen, and herb garden are reconstructions of originals. Interpretive program and picnic facilities. Open daily, 9-5. (318-394-3754). Nearby is the famous Gabriel Oak.

CATAHOULA LAKE: La. 96, features excellent fishing, crawfishing, and crabbing. The unincorporated community of Catahoula is a small fishing village.

NEW IBERIA: "New Spain," the town was established in 1779 with the arrival of Francisco Bouligny and a group of Malaguenos in what is now the business district along Bayou Teche. The town was incorporated in 1813 and experienced growth during the steamboat era until 1943. **Iberia Parish Tourist Information Center,** junction of U.S. 90

and La. 14, offers information, maps, walking and driving guides, and brochures. (318-365-1540). **Shadows-on-the-Teche,** 117 E. Main, built in 1835, is a beautiful house museum and property of the National Trust. An outstanding example of a planter's town house, it is authentically restored and furnished. Open daily except holidays, 9-4:30. Admission. (318-369-6446). **Mintmere Plantation House,** 1400 E. Main, built in 1857, is a Greek Revival raised cottage, site of a Civil War skirmish. An early Acadian cottage, circa 1790, is on the grounds. Drive-by. **Maison Marceline,** 442 E. Main, built circa 1893, is an interesting example of Eastlake Victorian architecture, open by appt. Admission. **Statue of Hadrian,** Weeks at St. Peters, is a Roman sculpture, A.D. 130, of the Emperor Hadrian. **Gebert Oak,** 541 E. Main, planted in 1831 over the grave of a young boy, is a member of the Live Oak Society. **Episcopal Church of the Epiphany,** 303 W. Main, the oldest church still in use in New Iberia, was consecrated in 1858. Used during the Civil War as a field hospital and prison. By appt. **Konriko Rice Mill,** 307 Ann, is the nation's oldest working rice mill. Slide shows, tours, crafts, and indigenous food. Open Mon.-Sat., 9-5. Admission. (318-367-6163).

Trappey's Factory tour offers tours of the food processing plant and bottling operation. Weekdays, 9-2:30; Friday, 9-1. Admission. (318-365-8281). **City Park,** on 45 acres in the center of town on the north bank of Bayou Teche, offers recreation facilities and boat launch and is the site of the **Louisiana Sugar Cane Festival and Fair.** Held the last weekend in September, it opens with the blessing of the cane fields. Exhibits represent 17 sugar-growing parishes, entertainment, art, fais-do-do, parades. **Justine Plantation,** La. 86, 4 miles east, built in 1822 of cypress construction but added on to in the 1890s. House features furnishings from several periods and a bottle collection. By appt. (318-364-0973)

SPANISH LAKE: La. 182, known for bass fishing, originally formed out of an oxbow of Bayou Teche, with four plantation houses located on its banks. Public boat launch.

LAKE FAUSSE POINTE STATE PARK: located off the West Atchafalaya Protection Levee Road, on Lake Fausse Pointe, a beautiful 15,000-acre, cypress-fringed lake. The park occupies 6,000 acres between the levee and Bayou Teche in a wilderness. Cabins, camping, nature trails, fishing, canoe rentals available. Admission. (318-229-4764). Airboat swamp rides. Fee. **Suggested scenic drive:** the West Atchafalaya Protection Levee Road from La. 3083 to Charenton.

CYPREMORT POINT: La. 319 is a scenic, curving, treelined drive to **Cypremort Point,** which means "dead cypress point." This is one of

Louisiana's best, most accessible Gulf beaches and the only one between Grand Isle and Cameron that can be reached by car. Public beach and camping. **Cypremort Point State Park** on 185 acres offers swimming, sailing, picnicking, pier fishing in Vermilion Bay, and marsh viewing. (318-367-4510)

JEANERETTE: La. 182, an Acadian town on both sides of Bayou Teche, with antebellum homes (most private, drive-by) lining the road. **Jeanerette Chamber of Commerce,** located at the Jeanerette Museum, 500 Main, offers information, maps, and brochures. (318-276-4293). **Jeanerette Museum,** 500 Main, houses exhibits about sugarcane history, country kitchen and farm equipment, natural history, and local culture. Open weekdays, 9-5. Admission. (318-276-4408). **Jeanerette Canal and Boat Ramp** provides access to Lake Fausse Pointe. **Albania,** La. 182 east, built 1837-42, is surrounded by moss-draped oaks. Drive-by. **Scenic drive:** along La. 182 west from Jeanerette to New Iberia.

CHARENTON: La. 326, **Jean Lafitte National Historical Park, Chitimacha Unit,** is on the site of the only Federally recognized Indian reservation in the state. The reservation is on 283 acres of original homeland. The Tribal Museum displays a variety of Chitimacha baskets, artifacts, and cultural and historical items relating the tribe. Open Mon.-Fri., 8-4:30. (318-923-4830)

ATTAKAPAS ISLAND WILDLIFE MANAGEMENT AREA: accessible by boat, this 25,000-acre tract of swampland in the Atchafalaya Basin offers hunting, fishing, some bird-watching. (318-942-7553)

BALDWIN: An important lumber and sugar community in the 1800s with several significant homes, including Darby, circa 1827, one of the best examples of French Louisiana Colonial architecture (now a bank), Tillandsia, and Heaton House, the authentic restoration of a small, Italian, 19th-century-inspired villa. Private, drive-by.

FRANKLIN: founded in 1808 on the banks of Bayou Teche and named parish seat in 1811, the town was first settled predominantly by Englishmen from the Atlantic coast. **The Franklin National Register Historic District** includes numerous buildings, many from the original mid-19th-century town along the banks of Bayou Teche, and is considered one of the most picturesque in Acadiana. La. 182 through Franklin is a scenic route. **Oaklawn Manor,** Irish Bend Road, a 3-story, Greek Revival mansion built in 1837, was the manor house of a large sugar plantation. Open Mon.-Sat., 10-4. Admission. (318-828-0434). **Grevemberg House Museum,** La. 322 off W. Main, built of cypress about 1851 in Greek Revival style, displays St. Mary Parish Museum exhibits. Open Thurs.-Sun., 10-4. Admission. (318-828-2092). **Arlington**

Plantation, 56 E. Main, Greek Revival style built in 1861 on a Spanish land grant, is carefully restored with period furnishing. By appt. Admission. (318-828-2644). **Bocage,** built in the mid-19th century in Greek Revival style, was transported by barge from its original site. Drive-by. Many other plantation homes in the area are also private, but well worth a drive-by. **St. Mary's Episcopal Church,** 805 First, completed in 1872 to replace the 1849 church that burned. The marble font was saved. **Asbury Methodist Church,** originally built in 1838 for a Baptist congregation and renovated in 1970. **St. Mary Bank & Trust building,** 614 Main, constructed in 1898 in classic Victorian commercial style and completely renovated to that elegance.

CENTERVILLE: an area of sugarcane commerce during the steamboat era. **Joshua Cary House,** in Centerville at La. 182 and 317, is a large cypress antebellum house in the Greek Revival style constructed with pegs, notches, and square nails. Drive-by. Other interesting, but private, buildings are: Shakespeare Allen House, built circa 1850, with a center pediment supported by four fluted Corinthian columns; Kennedy Hotel, built before 1855 of simple cypress construction, now a bank; Vitter House, built in 1850 in Greek Revival style; Presbyterian Church, built in 1879, set in a grove of live oaks.

PATTERSON: site of the Battle of Bisland (historical marker) and Patterson Airport, one of the south's most complete airports in the 1930s because of the aviation activities of Jimmie Wedell, pilot and designer, and Harry Williams, lumberman and promoter. **Wedell-Williams Memorial Aviation Museum of Louisiana,** La. 182, on Wedell and Williams' old airstrip, is dedicated to preserving Louisiana's aviation history. Artifacts and memorabilia of Wedell and Williams, as well as changing exhibits. Open Tues.-Sat., 10-4. Admission. (504-395-7067). **Swamp tours** available in the area. **Kemper Williams Park,** a 290-acre recreation facility, offers picnicking, tennis courts, driving range, baseball fields, and nature trail. **Scenic drive:** La. 182 from Patterson to Franklin.

MORGAN CITY: on the banks of the Atchafalaya River, on the site of the Tiger Island Sugar Plantation, the town was incorporated as Brashear City in 1860, then renamed for Charles Morgan, a New York businessman who centered his steamship and railroad activities here. It was the westernmost end of the Union Army supply line in the Civil War. In 1947, Kerr-McGee's rig 16 struck oil in the open Gulf, beginning the offshore oil industry. **St. Mary Parish Tourist Commission,** 112 Main, offers tourist information, maps, and brochures. Open 8-5. (504-395-4905). **Morgan City Tourist Information Center,** 725 Myrtle, offers information, maps, and brochures. Open daily, 9-4. (504-

384-3343). **Swamp Gardens,** 725 Myrtle, is a natural heritage museum in a natural swamp setting, with displays and guided tours along raised pathways, to show man's struggle for survival in the Atchafalaya Basin. Alligators, an 800-year-old cypress tree, and an authentically furnished cypress houseboat constructed in the early 1900s are of special interest. Tours daily. (Buy tickets at tourist center.) Also **Original Swamp Gardens** featuring native wildlife and guided walking tour. Open daily. **St. Mary Arts & Humanities Council** offers information on special exhibits, performances, and events. (318-384-7644). **Spirit of Morgan City,** La. 182, features a shrimp boat placed on the neutral ground of the highway to commemorate the shrimpers' discovery of jumbo shrimp in the 1930s. **Eternal Flame,** La. 182, serves as a monument to the offshore oil industry.

Brownell Memorial Park, La. 70 at Lake Palourde, is a 9.5-acre park that offers picnicking among the diverse plantlife, such as cypress trees, palmettos, elephant ears, ferns, and other native wild plants that grow along swamp ridges. The Brownell Carillon Tower houses 61 bronze bells cast in Holland. Open weekdays, 9-4; weekends, 9-7. **Lake Palourde,** La. 70 north, is a large natural lake with moss-draped oaks and cypress, offering fishing, sailing, and boating. Lake End Park on the northwest side has picnicking facilities, beach, camping, and fishing. (504-385-2160). **Turn of the Century House,** 715 Second, is a fine example of a Victorian home containing interesting artifacts, Mardi Gras costumes, and memorabilia. Also viewings of the silent movie *Tarzan of the Apes* and *Thunder Bay,* both filmed in Morgan City. Open Mon.-Fri., 9-4:30, Admission. (504-380-4651). **The Great Wall,** Front Street, a 21-foot-tall retaining or flood wall for the Atchafalaya River, offers a view of the water traffic. The Atchafalaya, when it receives Mississippi River overflow as redirected by the Old River control structure (see central Louisiana), empties past Morgan City into the Gulf. **Swamp and marsh tours** are offered by boat or seaplane. Inquire at tourist centers. **Shrimp and Petroleum Festival,** held Labor Day weekend, features sports, arts and crafts, parades, street dances, food, an ecumenical festival mass, and the blessing of the shrimp fleet in Berwick Bay. (504-385-0703). **Bayou Bass Challenge** held in June features professional fishermen and National Football League players, a fais-do-do, and other festivities.

ATCHAFALAYA DELTA WILDLIFE MANAGEMENT AREA: located at the mouth of the Atchafalaya as it empties into the Gulf, the 126,000-acre tract is accessible only by boat. The marsh habitat is good for hunting. Primitive camping. (504-568-5885)

Unique Louisiana

COURIR DE MARDI GRAS

Chicken chasing, Cajun music, and community gumbo may lack the glamor of the glossy urban rituals that New Orleans and Lafayette call Mardi Gras, but the Courir de Mardi Gras (literally, the Run of Mardi Gras) is a version of the Fat Tuesday celebration that offers its own unique country spirit.

Though a variety of prairie towns from Ville Platte and Eunice to tiny L'Anse Maigre and Soileau host a country Mardi Gras, the Courir in Mamou (population 3,200) is among the best organized and most colorful in the area. Revived and restructured in 1952 after a long hiatus, the Mamou Mardi Gras is part ritual, part street party, with much revelry and costume. The run is open to any male over seventeen with spirit enough to pay the entry fee, hang onto his saddle, and promise not to carry a weapon. And for everyone else, Cajun music and street-dancing in the middle of town create a festival atmosphere long before the riders return.

Just after 6:30 A.M., in front of the American Legion Hall in what passes for downtown Mamou, the Mardi Gras gathers, a swarming contingent of clown suits and satin cowboy outfits, be-hatted and masked in rigs from clever to demonic. Some participants mount their horses with a nonchalance derived mainly from breakfast beer; a few without horses hop aboard a tractor-driven wagon. The Capitaines, unmasked and wearing buff-colored cowboy hats and purple and gold capes of responsibility, mingle among the riders, anxiously anticipating a full day of sheep-dogging the 100 uninhibited participants.

It is a parade in the most informal sense as it clops lazily out of town along country roads that slice through the flat, winter farmland. Accompanied by a live Cajun band riding a makeshift float, the paraders' chank-a-chank anthems can be heard long before their arrival. Spectators line the roads, clotting thickly in front of houses where the Courir de Mardi Gras stops.

The ostensible mission of the courir is to gather ingredients for the community gumbo, which is made and served back at Legion Hall. *"Voulez-vous recevoir cette bande de Mardi Gras?"* (Do you want to receive this gang of Mardi Gras?) the captain asks when he approaches a farmhouse. If the answer is yes, a flap of his white flag signals the riders to spur their horses down the driveway. Whooping and hollering, they dismount and chase the farmer's offering—one or more fleeing, fluttering chickens which, contrary to popular belief, are not dead and packaged, but very much alive and feathered at the outset. After each victorious chicken chase, the riders dance among themselves, occasionally with a bystander, or even a horse, try to kiss pretty girls, perform acrobatics on horseback, and take painless pratfalls, all in time to the melodious tunes from fiddle, accordion, and washboard.

By late morning, the tail of the parade has grown to a mile-long caravan of cars, trucks, motorcycles, ATVs, and bikes that follows the riders from house to house, stopping when the parade stops, pressing on in its wake, and adding dubiously to the festive chaos.

In town, the aroma of gumbo has begun to waft from the Legion Hall kitchen, and the bandstand erected in the center of town is the centerpiece for an ever-growing street party. Costumed revellers and curious visitors packed for several blocks in every direction entertain themselves dancing, picnicking, and milling about downtown Mamou.

By midafternoon, the bedraggled courir reappears in town, triumphantly dismounting to dance like heroes before the bandstand, then heading for Legion Hall to demand their share of gumbo. A Mardi Gras dance and costume party follows, open to all and lasting until the clock strikes midnight. Then, like Cinderella's Ball, the party's over and the Mardi Gras revellers are transformed into penitents for Lent.

But no one can argue. The Courir de Mardi Gras is, after all, a performance that couldn't be repeated two days in a row.

Unique Louisiana

CRAWFISH FARMING

A man in hip boots wades through a large, square pond, pulling a galvanized wash tub behind him. He stops every so often to lift a wire basket from the water and dump its contents into his tub, then continues along, repeating the rhythmic, mechanical movement that seems half assembly line, half ballet, in the knee-deep pool.

It's nearly the same process in a much larger waterhole where two men, separated by a grid of low levees, are making the same odd movements. But one paddles a rowboat and the other sits in a flatboat that follows a metal wheel rolling ahead of it, seemingly pulling the craft along through the shallow water. The pond is dotted with plastic caps laid in parallel, slightly-swerving rows from one end to the other, and the men are engaged in the same pull-up-and-dump routine as the wader, upending the plastic-capped, wire contraption to empty its contents, then placing a biscuit-size nugget into the basket before tossing it in again, in one continuous, well-threaded motion. Every so often, the men heave several bulging, orange mesh bags onto the levee bank.

This activity that looks like trapping and smells like fishing is crawfish farming, or, in technological parlance, aquaculture—the pond cultivation of the crustacean delicacy traditionally available only in the wild.

Not long ago, edible crawfish—called, with deprecatory affection, "mudbugs"—were caught in the Atchafalaya Basin, sometime between April and June, by fishermen in motorboats or poling a pirogue deep into the winding, cypress-shaded channels of the swamp. Every year, Basin fishermen—and mudbug fanciers—would pray for a deep enough level on the Butte LaRose gauge in late March to promise a bumper crop. Native crawfish that burrowed in farmers' fields were regarded as nuisances.

Then, through the ingenuity of researchers at Louisiana State, Southern and Southwestern Louisiana universities, the concept developed of turning the lowly crawfish into an agricultural industry—to create a more dependable, larger, and more accessible catch by

97

controlling the conditions under which they could be raised, effecting a much longer harvest season. Currently, roughly one hundred thousand acres in south Louisiana are devoted to crawfish farming.

Mudbug aquaculture begins with digging a pond or flooding a rice field, seeding it with red crawfish—unless the native white species is acceptable—and nurturing their growth through proper feeding, water circulation, and protection. In effect, creating an environment that allows the mudbugs to live their natural cycle in a climate even more favorable than the Basin. Then, much earlier and for a longer period of time, the resulting crop is lured into traps and hauled to a boiler, a broker, or a processor.

Like many fledgling industries, crawfish farming's techniques are not yet uniform. Which is why some farmers still catch their crop the old-fashioned way, by wading or poling a pirogue and baiting homemade traps with dead fish, while others rely on the most up-to-date research and state-of-the-art equipment—scientifically processed pellet bait, hydraulic-powered boats created just for the shallow draft of crawfish ponds, engineer-designed traps, and functionally aerated water systems. Regardless of method, however, their goal is identical: catch as many forty-pound bags of the little critters as possible.

The mystique of crawfish farming is easily shared. This is due, in part, to the character of the crawfish farmer—often a Cajun, by birth or by nature—who, with a twinkle in his eye, can entertain a listener with the same tales about crawfish that crawfishermen have always told. All the while grabbing and dumping and sinking those little wire cages that look something like three tennis racquet heads tacked together under a plastic collar.

And then, there's a certain charm in the idea of planting and harvesting a freshwater crustacean that waves menacing pincers and darts off backwards in a movement which has inspired the vernacular expression, "he's crawfishin'," meaning "to wiggle out of a situation."

Surely, few other farmers can boast crops with such personality!

Crawfish farming. (Photograph by Mary Ann Sternberg)

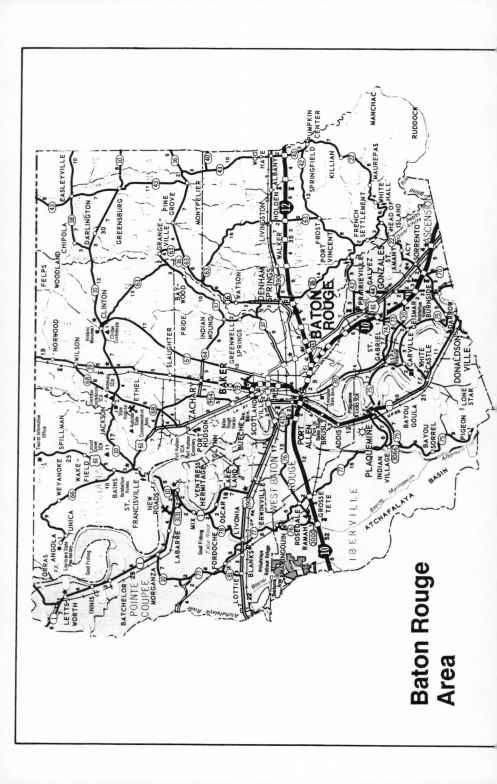

Baton Rouge
Area

6

Baton Rouge
and Its Environs

The French explored much of this area in the 17th century, and their strong influence remains. Bienville, in fact, noted a red boundary marker dividing the land of two Indian tribes as he wended his way along the Mississippi River and cited the "baton rouge," or red stick, in his journal. Acadians settled between the Mississippi and Atchafalaya rivers. The Spanish controlled the area for a time as well, and even English influence was felt in the Felicianas. When much of the area was not included in the Louisiana Purchase, but was deeded to Spain, a group of local citizens rebelled and, in 1810, for 74 days established the independent West Florida Republic, which then became part of the United States.

The Republic of West Florida included the territory from the Mississippi River east to the Mississippi state line and from the state boundary on the north to a line approximately across the top of Lake Maurepas. Parishes in Baton Rouge and environs are Pointe Coupee, West Feliciana, East Feliciana, St. Helena, Livingston, East Baton Rouge, West Baton Rouge, Iberville, and Ascension. Baton Rouge, the capital of Louisiana, is the largest city.

POINTE COUPEE: the name of the parish is derived from the natural cut-off or "cut point" that the Mississippi River made, cutting off what is now False River to form a more direct route.

INNIS: off La. 1 is the site of **St. Stephen's Episcopal Church,** a Gothic Revival building constructed in 1850-58 and consecrated by "Fighting Bishop" Leonidas Polk. The cemetery contains Confederate graves. Tour by appt. (504-492-3534)

OLD RIVER LOCKS: at Lettsworth, is part of the flood control structure mentioned in Chapter 1. **Old River** is a Mississippi River ox-bow prized for fishing.

MORGANZA SPILLWAY: at Morganza, is part of the flood control structure to channel an overflow into the Atchafalaya Basin.

(NOTE: The text now crosses to the east bank of the Mississippi River. However, to continue south along the west bank of the river, please skip to FALSE RIVER AREA in this chapter for contiguous attractions.)

ANGOLA: on the east side of the Mississippi River and the western end of the scenic Tunica Trace, La. 66, which begins at Bains and me-anders through hilly, wooded countryside dotted with historic sites and buildings. The state's maximum security prison is on the site of Angola Plantation. On the nearby bluffs overlooking the Mississippi River a Jesuit missionary with Iberville had the local Indians construct a chapel in 1700, the first Catholic church in the lower Mississippi River Valley. **The Angola Rodeo** is held Sunday afternoons in October. Riding, roping, other rodeo events. Admission.

TUNICA: La. 66, located on the banks of the Mississippi River and named for the Tunica Indian tribe. Nearby was found the Tunica Trea-sure, an extraordinary collection of Indian and European artifacts ex-cavated from burial mounds. The remnants of the Tunica tribe now live near Marksville. (Refer to Chapter 3.)

WEST FELICIANA/ST. FRANCISVILLE: John James Audubon called West Feliciana "Happy Land," Americanizing the Spanish trans-lation of Feliciana to describe the wooded, fertile, hilly, and historic area he painted in the 1820s. Though changed since Audubon's day, much of the atmosphere he enjoyed still exists. Several back roads of-fer especially picturesque drives, and many plantation homes remain. The **West Feliciana Parish Tourist Commission,** 364 Ferdinand in St. Francisville, is housed with the West Feliciana Historical Society in a Greek Revival hardware store and offers information on the area, spe-cial tours, maps, and brochures. Open Mon.-Sat., 9-4; Sun., 1-4. (504-635-3743). **Live Oak Plantation,** in Weyanoke, one of the earliest houses in the Felicianas, dates from circa 1808 and reflects Spanish architectural influence. The house, beautifully restored and furnished to reflect its history, is reached through a lane of massive live oaks, planted in the 1830s. Open by appt. Admission. (504-638-9004). **St. Mary's Episcopal Church,** on La. 66 near Weyanoke, founded in 1854 as a country mission by Grace Episcopal Church. The small brick Gothic church is no longer in use.

Greenwood Plantation, near Weyanoke, was originally built in 1830, survived the Civil War, and was destroyed by fire in 1960. From the remains of 28 Doric columns, the house has been reconstructed. Recently used for several movies and made-for-TV specials, the grounds are dotted with outbuildings and effects designed for the films. Open Mon.-Sat., 10-4; Sun., 11-5. Admission. (504-655-4475). **Highland Plantation,** off La. 66 on Highland Road, built circa 1804 on a Spanish land grant using local materials and excellent craftsmanship, has remained in the same family and contains many of the original furnishings. An oak-shaded, brick-walled family cemetery is on the grounds. By appt. Admission. (504-635-3001). **McCausland Cemetery,** La. 967 east of U.S. 61, is a tiny plot of bordered brick walkways surrounded by a wrought-iron fence that holds graves dating from the early 1800s. **The Cottage Plantation,** on U.S. 61, built on a 1795 Spanish land grant on a bluff over Alexander's Creek, incorporates English-style early additions to the original simple Spanish structure. Many of the original plantation outbuildings remain. Open daily, 9-5. Admission. (504-635-3674)

Catalpa Plantation, on U.S. 61, is a late Victorian raised cottage, not the first residence on this site, on a parklike landscape, some of which is antebellum. Open daily except Dec.-Jan. by appt. Admission. (504-635-3372). **Afton Villa Gardens,** U.S. 61, on part of Spanish land grant from 1790s, are the formal landscaped gardens that survived a fire in the 1960s that destroyed the elaborate home completed in 1857. Gardens open March-Oct. Admission. (504-635-6773). **Rosedown Plantation and Gardens** was built in 1835 by a wealthy cotton planter who modeled his 28 acres of landscaping after Versailles. Open daily, March-Oct., 9-5; Nov.-Feb., 10-5. Closed holidays. Admission. (504-635-3332). **Butler Greenwood** is an early-19th-century English cottage featuring an elaborate Civil War era parlor and extensive antebellum gardens. Tours daily, 9-5; Sun, 1-5. Admission. (504-635-6312). **Locust Grove State Commemorative Area,** east of U.S. 61 on Locust Grove Road, is on the site of Locust Grove Plantation, home of Jefferson Davis's sister. In the cemetery is buried Davis's first wife, Sarah, daughter of Zachary Taylor, and other area notables. Gates close. (504-635-3739)

Oakley House, Audubon State Commemorative Area, La. 965 east of U.S. 61, includes a 100-acre park with 2-mile trail into the natural landscaping surrounding the graceful, West Indies-style house, built in 1799. Painter/naturalist John James Audubon tutored here in 1821 and visited thereafter, painting many of his famous works. The home has been impeccably restored and furnished. Open daily, 9-5. Admission. (504-635-3739). **The Oaks,** U.S. 61, is a late-19th-century home with Victorian ornamentation set at the end of an avenue of stately

Grave of Sarah Knox Davis, first wife of Jefferson Davis, in Locust Grove Cemetery, St. Francisville. (Courtesy Louisiana Office of Tourism)

oaks. By appt. (504-635-3418). **The Myrtles,** U.S. 61, was built on a Spanish land grant in 1796; the addition of ornate iron grillwork on the front gallery and extensive remodeling took place in the mid-19th century. It is known for having ghosts. Open daily, 9-5. Admission. (504-635-6277). **Audubon Art Gallery,** U.S. 61 at hotel on lake, exhibits an entire edition of 435 Amsterdam prints of Audubon's Birds of America series with explication. Open daily, 9-5. **River Bend Energy Center,** La. 965 west of U.S. 61, contains an exhibit explicating energy, from Thomas Edison to nuclear power as it is produced at the nearby River Bend nuclear generating station. Open weekdays, 8-4. (504-635-5004). **Hebrew Rest Cemetery,** old Hwy. 61, established in 1891, records its first burial in 1895. The beautiful, oak-shaded cemetery surrounded by wrought-iron fencing is no longer used. **Thompson Creek,** forming the boundary between East and West Feliciana, is a beautiful, winding waterway with natural sand beaches, but may be dangerous in high water.

BAYOU SARA: in the late 1790s, between the Mississippi River and the bluff, the settlement of Bayou Sara was established. It became one of the most significant cotton ports on the river—in 1850, the largest between New Orleans and Memphis—and was shelled and torched during the Civil War. But the coming of the railroad and the decline of the cotton industry brought about the end of Bayou Sara's commercial success. Fire and a Mississippi River flood finally destroyed it altogether. The St. Francisville-New Roads ferry now lands at the former site of Bayou Sara.

ST. FRANCISVILLE: the town grew as a result of the Capuchin cemetery that was established in 1785 on the high land overlooking the Mississippi River. This large National Register Historic District contains many 19th-century buildings. **West Feliciana Historical Society Museum,** 364 Ferdinand, housed in a hardware store and blacksmithery built in 1896, exhibits area history and artifacts. The tourist information center in this building offers maps and visitor information. Open Mon.-Sat., 9-4; Sun., 1-4. (504-635-6330). **Mary Pipes Butler Memorial Garden,** next door to the museum, is a pocket garden with brick walkways and native plants, as well as cultivated materials. **Grace Episcopal Church,** 480 Ferdinand, is an English Gothic-style church built in 1858, replacing an earlier, smaller church—the second oldest Episcopal church in Louisiana, started in 1828. It was shelled and badly damaged during the Civil War. The cemetery is shaded by oaks planted in 1855. **Law Offices,** 116 Prosperity Street, were built in 1842 to house lawyers and have always been used as such. Private. Among historic townhouses, Propinquity, 523 Royal, by appt., admission (504-635-6540), and the Wolf-Schlesinger House, 118 N. Commerce, a Victorian Gothic home from 1880, can be toured; drive-by others. **Audubon Pilgrimage,** mid-March, offers the opportunity to tour many of the private homes, plantations, and other historic buildings. Admission. Demonstrations of 19th-century skills and crafts at the Rural Homestead. (504-635-6330)

PORT HUDSON: Port Hudson State Commemorative Area, U.S. 61, is a 650-acre park commemorating the important Battle of Port Hudson, spring of 1862, when the Union Army gained control of the Mississippi River following one of the bloodiest sieges of the war. Six miles of hiking trails visit the sites of the skirmishes. Fort Desperate is handicapped-accessible. Battlefield museum features artifacts and interpretive program. Picnic facilities. Civil War Living History reenactment—third weekend in March. (504-654-3775). **Port Hudson National Cemetery,** La. 3133 west of U.S. 61, contains graves of Confederate and Union soldiers and veterans from later conflicts.

JACKSON: named for Gen. Andrew Jackson, who camped on the banks of nearby Thompson Creek after his victory at the Battle of New Orleans. The town was established in 1815 and was the original seat of the parish of Feliciana until 1824 when a division created East and West Felicianas. A large National Register Historic District, it incorporates many fine old buildings. Those not open to the public can be viewed as drive-bys. **East Louisiana State Hospital,** a monumental Greek Revival-style public facility for the mentally ill, was constructed in 1854 under the legislative dictum to not look like a prison. Open weekdays, 9-4. **East Feliciana Parish Courthouse,** completed in 1817, is no longer used as a courthouse. **Milbank,** 102 Bank, a Greek Revival-style residence used later commercially, now restored as a residence, was built in 1836. Open daily, 10-4. Tours. Admission. (504-634-5901). **Centenary College,** E. College, includes a Greek Revival west wing built in 1837, the only one of three wings to survive. During the Civil War it was used as a hospital and military barracks. Drive-by. **Jackson Methodist Church,** Bank Street, was built in 1852 and features an unusual square bell tower. **Jackson First Baptist Church,** built in 1860, was used to hide Confederate troops and their horses from the Union Army. **St. Alban's Masonic Lodge,** Bank Street, built in 1826, houses the post office on the first floor. **Presbyterian Church,** Bank Street, built in 1852, has a stairway up to the former slaves' gallery. **Roseneath,** Bank at Erin, built in 1832, is a Greek Revival 2-story frame house. Drive-by. **West Florida Republic Museum,** College Street north of La. 10, displays a variety of artifacts and memorabilia of the West Florida Republic heritage, including domestic furnishings, weaponry, dugout pirogues, and Indian artifacts. Tues.-Sun., 10-5. (504-634-7155). **Jackson Assembly Antique Show and Sale,** held the last weekend in March, includes a driving tour of historic area and country foods. **Asphodel Plantation,** on La. 68 south of Jackson, is a 14-room house with Doric columns built in 1820, and surrounded by beautiful grounds. By appt. Admission. (504-654-8481). **Asphodel Village,** near Asphodel Plantation, includes the Levy house, circa 1850, which was moved to the site, plantation cottages, and nature trail. (504-654-6868)

SLAUGHTER: known as Belzara until the Slaughter family donated land for the railroad in 1888. A number of interesting late Victorian houses, including two rows of four-in-a-row, are here.

CLINTON: established in 1824 as the parish seat, it became the legal and educational center of the area and boasts a large concentration of Greek Revival structures. **East Feliciana Parish Tourist Commission** offers information, maps and brochures, tours. (504-634-7155). **East Feliciana Courthouse,** a Greek Revival structure built in 1840, is unusual for its octagonal cupola on a leaded slate roof. Open weekdays, 8-4:30. **Lawyers' Row,** facing the rear of courthouse, is a row of Greek Revival buildings built from 1840 to 1860, used for lawyers' offices. One building houses the Audubon Regional Library. **Brame-Bennett House,** built in 1840 of Greek temple architecture, is open by appt. (504-683-5241). **Marston House,** built in 1837 as a combination bank and house, still has the original vault. By appt. Admission. (504-683-5594). **St. Andrew's Church,** built in 1842, is a Victorian-Gothic Episcopal church. By appt. **Woodside,** a small Gothic cottage built in 1847, is open by appt. **Bonnie Burn,** on Woodville Road, is a Greek Revival home, built in 1858 and restored in the 1960s. By appt. **Clinton Confederate Cemetery** is 4-acre cemetery with Civil War burials from both sides. **Feliciana Peach Festival,** celebrating the south Louisiana peach crop, takes place the third weekend in June. Arts and crafts, food, entertainment. **East Feliciana Pilgrimage,** with headquarters at Marston House, the third weekend in April, offers tours of historic homes. (504-683-8677)

WILSON: includes interesting examples of Victorian architecture. **Glencoe Plantation** was built in 1870 and entirely rebuilt in 1898 after a fire. Wide galleries, Victorian gingerbread and turrets, and decorative fish-scale shingles are among the home's interesting features. By appt. Admission. (504-629-5387). **Oakland Plantation,** La. 963, built in 1827, is a 3-story plantation house built in the Carolina I-type construction. By appt. (504-629-5960)

NORWOOD: established in 1883 on land donated to the railroad, offers many examples of both domestic and residential Victorian architecture, including Gableton and the Norwood Town Hall, formerly the Bank of Norwood, both built in 1890.

CHIPOLA: La. 38 and 432, is site of Chipola Motorcycle Trails and Moto Cross. A winding, wooded, and hilly trail. Closed Sunday A.M. (to avoid interfering with church services) and during hunting season. **Amite River,** west of Chipola, is a clear, shallow river that flows the length of St. Helena and Livingston parishes. Fishing, canoeing, and swimming. May be dangerous in high water. **Fluker's Bluff,** off La. 432, is an unusual land formation along the river, good for walking and picnicking. **Tickfaw River,** east of Chipola, runs from the north part of the parish into Lake Maurepas. Scenic river for fishing, tubing, canoeing, camping.

DARLINGTON: La. 448, is the site of the Wesley Chapel Methodist Church. Founded in 1855, this church was completed in 1890 and still contains its original handhewn pews.

GREENSBURG: Old Jail Museum on La. 10, is housed in the St. Helena Parish Jail, built in 1855 adjacent to the courthouse square, featuring history and memorabilia of the parish. By appt. (504-777-4365). **Land Office Building,** completed circa 1820, is a Greek Revival structure that served as a clearing house for the sale of all public land between the Mississippi and Pearl rivers north of New Orleans until the office was moved to Baton Rouge in 1843. St. Helena Forest Festival is held the last Saturday in September.

ALBANY: on U.S. 190, is the oldest Hungarian settlement in the nation which has kept its cultural heritage and traditions alive. **Hungarian Harvest Festival** is held the first weekend in October. Arts and crafts, food, cultural heritage.

HOLDEN: Fontenot's Trading Post Museum, N. Doyle Road, features Civil War and Indian exhibits and artifacts. Open daily, 9-5. (504-686-2965)

LIVINGSTON: 5 miles northeast of town is the Macedonia Baptist Church, a primitive-style church built in 1898 and still in use. **Livingston Parish Fair,** held the second weekend in October, is an old-time country fair, featuring 4-H livestock competition, wagon train parade, carnival, music, entertainment, and food.

WALKER: called the Pine Tree Capital of the World, the town was settled in 1861. **The Pine Tree Festival** is held first weekend in May. **The Old South Jamboree,** a live country music show, is held alternate Saturday nights. Admission.

SPRINGFIELD: the oldest incorporated community in the parish was once a lumber boomtown. **Springfield Courthouse,** off La. 22, was built in 1832 as a colonial home that was used as the first courthouse when the parish was established. **Scenic drive:** La. 43 from Springfield north to Greensburg follows the Old Lousiana Turnpike, an early toll road.

DENHAM SPRINGS: in 1827, William Denham discovered mineral springs nearby and the village became a health resort. **Headquarters for the National Association of Louisiana Catahoulas,** Louisiana's official and only native canine. Museum and information. NALC Spring Dog Show, the last Sunday in March. **Thunderbird Beach,** open summer through Labor Day, features a lake, beach, and rides. Admission.

FRENCH SETTLEMENT/HEAD OF ISLAND/PORT VINCENT: settled in 1800 by French, German, and Italian emigrés who arrived via the Amite River. Cypress sawmills, shingle-making, and steamboat service were once the area's mainstays. Today, these tiny communities are fishing villages. Louisiana's "First Cajun," Justin Wilson, lives near French Settlement. **The Creole House Museum,** La. 16 behind Town Hall, is a Creole-style cottage built in 1898 containing antiques, photographs, genealogical records, memorabilia, and artifacts of the original settlers of La Côte Française, the French Coast. Open the third Sunday of each month, 2-4 P.M. and by appt. (504-698-6114). A swamp walkway and tours available from Bayview Tavern.

RIVER ROAD: the east bank River Road is one of two scenic roads that follow the Mississippi River along each side. The levee separates the roads physically and visually from the river. Along the roads are picturesque homes, historic plantations, and commercial buildings. A few of the homes and plantations are open to the public; many are private, but interesting drive-bys. Rural farmland and enormous industrial plants are neighbors. West bank River Road attractions in this area are listed later in this chapter, Port Allen to Donaldsonville. To continue south on the River Road, both east and west banks, see Chapter 8, Greater New Orleans.

BURNSIDE: The Cabin, La. 44 at La. 22, is a slave cabin from Monroe Plantation, built about 1830, that has been restored and used as a restaurant entrance. Open daily. **The Hermitage,** on River Road east of Darrow, built in 1812, is an example of classical revival style with Doric columns. Open for groups only. By appt. (504-891-8493). **Tezcuco Plantation,** on River Road near Darrow, built in 1855, is a restored Greek Revival-style raised cottage constructed of local materials. Ornately decorated with wrought iron and plaster frieze work and medallions. Open daily, 10-4. Admission. (504-562-3929). **Houmas House,** constructed in the late 18th century, was greatly altered and enlarged in 1840 to its present imposing Greek Revival plantation. Restored and furnished in the period. Open for tours daily, Feb.-Oct., 10-5; Nov.-Jan.,10-4. Admission. (504-473-7841). **Ashland-Belle Helene,** near Geismar, is among the romantic ruins of antebellum plantations open to the public. Currently undergoing restoration. This massive, Greek Revival home was begun in 1837 and completed in 1841, designed by famed New Orleans architect James Gallier. Extensive grounds. Open for tours daily, 9-5, except holidays. Admission. (504-473-1328)

GONZALES: earliest settlers of this community were the Houmas Indians. In 1887, Joseph ("Tee Joe") Gonzales established a post office, later subdividing and plotting the town. **The Tee Joe Gonzales Museum,** 728 N. Ascension, in the old railroad depot, contains vintage photos, silver, tools, antique furniture, and paintings relating to Ascension Parish history. Open Wed.-Fri., 1-5. The **Gonzales Tourist Information Center** is also housed here for information, maps, and brochures. (504-664-6000). **St. Theresa of Avila Catholic Church** was built in 1918 and is still in use. **Jambalaya Festival,** featuring a jambalaya cook-off, arts and crafts, and entertainment, is held the second weekend in June.

CARVILLE: La. 75, site of the National Hansen's Disease Center, the only hospital in the United States devoted to the treatment of leprosy patients. Its administration is housed in the whitewashed brick **Indian Camp** plantation house, built in the 1850s. Tours of the facility available. (504-642-7771)

ST. GABRIEL: on La. 75, is the site of the **St. Gabriel Catholic Church,** a steepled, weatherboard structure dating from the 1770s built by Acadian exiles. The church is no longer in use. The original bell is said to have been given by the Queen of Spain. It is the oldest Catholic church in the state. (504-642-8441). **Home Place Plantation,** on River Road, built in 1791 with briquette-entre-poteaux construction in the Louisiana Colonial style. By appt. (504-783-2123)

BAYOU MANCHAC: once the northern border of the Isle of Orleans and an important trade route linking the Mississippi River with Lake Maurepas, this bayou now is a quiet waterway that no longer flows into the Mississippi River.

BATON ROUGE: if the English had discovered the area first, the community might have been called Red Stick, instead of the French "baton rouge," which it was dubbed after Iberville noted the Indian boundary marker. The English did establish Fort New Richmond, which was captured by Bernardo de Galvez in the First Battle of Baton Rouge in 1779. The Second Battle of Baton Rouge occurred in 1862 during the Civil War. Baton Rouge is the seat of state government and the home of Louisiana's flagship public university. **Baton Rouge Area Convention and Visitors Bureau,** 838 North Boulevard, offers information, maps, brochures, and tour contacts. Open weekdays, 8:30-5 (504-383-1825). **Louisiana Tourist Information,** State Capitol, Memorial Hall. Open Mon.-Sat., 8:30-4; Sun., 1-4. **The Arts & Humanities Council of Greater Baton Rouge,** 427 Laurel, offers information on special exhibits, performances, and events. (504-344-8558)

The Foundation for Historical Louisiana, 900 North Boulevard, offers information on historic sites and districts and preservation. Tours. (504-387-2464). **Louisiana State Capitol,** built by Huey Long in 1931-32, is 34 stories tall, the tallest capitol in the nation. An observation tower on the 27th floor offers a spectacular view of the surrounding area. The capitol is built in the Art Deco style, with marble and bronze detailing. Tours given. A tourist information center is located in Memorial Hall, the main entrance. In the capitol basement breezeway is a permanent exhibit, The Creole State, with artifacts and explication of Louisiana's diverse folklife cultures. Open 8-4:30. **State Capitol Grounds** includes a statue of Huey Long and his gravesite, and extensive landscaped gardens. **Old Arsenal Museum,** on the capitol grounds, was built in 1835 as a powder magazine serving the nearby fort. Open Mon.-Sat., 10-4; Sun, 1-4. Admission. (504-387-2464). **Governor's Mansion,** off I-110 near the capitol, is a modified Greek Revival-style replica of a plantation house built in 1961. Downstairs public rooms open Mon.-Fri., 9-ll, 2-4. Reservations necessary. (504-342-5855)

Pentagon Barracks, Front Street near the capitol, built in 1823-24, is a group of four impressive Greek Revival structures used as U.S. Army barracks and also as dormitories for LSU cadets from 1886 to 1925. Zachary Taylor was among the famous men billeted here. The Foundation for Historical Louisiana Visitors Center, an interpretive center on the state capitol complex and related sites, is located in one of the buildings. Open daily, 10-4. (504-342-1866). **Site of Fort San Carlos,** near the Pentagon Barracks, is the location of the star-shaped Spanish fort that governed the West Florida parishes from 1779 to 1810, captured by the West Florida Republic insurrection in 1810. **Spanish Town,** the first formally planned Baton Rouge community, now an historic district, was laid out in 1805 by Don Carlos de Grandpre. Several early-to mid-19th-century homes still stand: Potts House, Grace-Persac House, Prescott-Dougherty House, Charlet House, Presbyterian Minister's Cottage. (504-342-1866). **Warden's House,** 703 Laurel, built 1837-40 in Georgian style, was used as living quarters

State Capitol, Baton Rouge. (Courtesy Louisiana Office of Tourism)

for the warden and his family and as a receiving station for state penitentiary prisoners. *Samuel Clemens* riverboat tours of the Baton Rouge harbor and Mississippi River. Tues.-Sun., at 10, 12, and 2 except January and February. Admission. (504-381-9606). **Lafayette Buildings,** Lafayette Street, are the sole remaining examples of late-18th-century architecture with iron columns and grillwork in the downtown area. The Marquis de Lafayette was entertained here in 1825 on his tour of America. **Old Water Tower,** built in 1888, is made of wrought iron and topped with an ornamental crest rail, the city's original and only water tower from 1888 to 1938.

Louisiana Arts and Science Center Riverside Museum, Front at North Boulevard, is housed in the 1925 Yazoo and Mississippi Valley Railroad depot. A permanent Egyptian exhibit, hands-on children's galleries for art and science exploration, and restored railroad cars are augmented by changing exhibits of fine arts, history, and science. Regularly scheduled astronomy programs. Good river overlook. Open Tues.-Fri., 10-3; Sat., 10-4; Sun., 1-4. Admission. (344-5272). **Old State Capitol,** North Boulevard at Front, an imposing neo-Gothic castle built in 1849 that served as the statehouse until 1932. The building was restored in 1882 after a disastrous fire and features a black and white marble foyer with grand iron spiral staircase. Reopening as the Louisiana Center of Political and Governmental History in 1993. **Riverfront Plaza,** a fountain and decorative area, with access to levee and Mississippi River overlook. **USS *Kidd/Nautical Historical Center*** features World War II Fletcher-class destroyer, restored to its V-J Day configuration. This 369-foot ship is berthed in a unique cradle that allows the ship to "float" in high water and to be studied from underneath in low water. The museum exhibits maritime and nautical artifacts and has a Louisiana veterans' memorial wall in its courtyard. Open daily, 9-5. Admission. (504-342-1942)

Catfish Town, a restored historic warehouse area, is the western end of Beauregard Town, a planned community laid out in 1806 on a baroque city plan by Elias Beauregard. Some mid-19th- and turn-of-the-century homes predominate, including Sutter House, 900 North Boulevard, headquarters for the Foundation for Historical Louisiana, Williams House, Fuqua House, and Beale House. **Old Governors Mansion,** 502 North Boulevard, built in 1930 by Huey Long, is furnished with fine Louisiana antiques and memorabilia from the governors. Open Sat., 10-4; Sun., 1-4. Admission. **Firefighter's Museum,** housed in the Old Bogan Fire Station, built in 1924, 427 Laurel, displays historic firefighting equipment, trucks, and artifacts. Open weekdays, 9-5:30. Upstairs is the Arts & Humanities Council of

Greater Baton Rouge gallery of changing exhibits. **St. Joseph's Cathedral,** 412 North Street, built in 1853, maintains an original exterior and a renovated interior. (504-387-5928). **St. James Episcopal Church,** a Gothic Revival-style church completed in 1895, counts among its founders Mrs. Zachary Taylor. (504-387-5928). **Magnolia Cemetery,** 19th at Laurel, established 1852-54, is a charming graveyard with 19th-century headstones. This was the site of the Battle of Baton Rouge in 1862.

Baton Rouge Gallery, in the Pavilion at City Park, is a nonprofit, professional gallery featuring changing exhibits. Open Tues.-Sat., 10-4. (504-383-1470). **Magnolia Mound Plantation,** 2161 Nicholson, built in 1796, is an historic house museum with interpretive programming and working, open-hearth kitchen representing south Louisiana culture from 1800 to 1830. Open Tues.-Sat., 10-4; Sun., 1-4. Special programs and festivals. Admission. (504-343-4955)

Louisiana State University, originally established in Pineville in 1860, moved to Baton Rouge in 1869. The present campus was dedicated in 1926 with the original buildings in Mediterranean style. Campus attractions include: *Anglo-American Art Museum,* in the base of Memorial Tower, contains paintings, silver, furnished rooms, and special exhibits reflecting the English influence on American culture. Open Mon.-Fri., 9-4; Sat., 10-12; Sun., 1-4. (504-388-4003). *Museum of Natural Science,* Foster Hall, contains dioramas of Louisiana wildlife scenes and mounted specimens of birds, reptiles, and other wildlife. (504-388-2855). *Museum of Geoscience,* in the Geology Building, features Dinotrek and changing exhibits in geology, anthropology, and geography. Open Sat., 10-5; Sun., 2-5; weekdays in summer. Admission. (504-388-GEOS). *Hill Memorial Library,* on the Quadrangle, exhibits rare books, paintings, documents, natural history and Louisiana collections, and special exhibits. Original, gracious, coffered-ceilinged, wood-panelled reading rooms are classic club style. *LSU Union Gallery,* in the LSU Union, offers changing exhibits of art and crafts. *Mike, the Tiger,* the LSU mascot, has a cage, next to the Assembly Center. For LSU campus information on sporting events, special exhibits and performances, call (504-388-3202). **Old Highland Cemetery,** established in 1815, is a tree-shaded, brick-walled, small parklike burial ground with historic markers and tombs, including that of Armand Duplantier and his wife Constance, who lived at Magnolia Mound. **Joseph Petitpierre House,** 5544 Highland, built in 1805, was moved to its current site and restored to its original condition, including paint colors and exposed bousillage wall. By appt. (504-766-2032). **University Lakes,** three small manmade lakes, offer in-town water recreation and bike paths. **Mt. Hope Plantation,** 8151 Highland, built circa 1817, is one of the few remaining farmhouse structures in the area. Drive-by.

Hilltop Arboretum, 11855 Highland Road, owned by LSU, consists of 12 rolling acres landscaped informally with a variety of native flora, labeled. Open daily, 8-5. Donations. (504-769-2363). **Kleinpeter House,** 18666 Perkins, is a 1 1/2-story frame, Greek Revival cottage set on the family's original plantation tract. Furnished with period pieces. By appt. Admission. (504-291-6649). **Rural Life Museum,** Essen Lane at I-10, owned by LSU, is a nationally recognized complex of 19th-century buildings, furnishings, and artifacts representing the usually unseen side of plantation life. Other period buildings are included as well as a barn/museum. Open Mon.-Fri., 8:30-4. Admission. (504-765-2437). Also on the grounds of **Burden Research Plantation** are test gardens for roses, annuals, perennials, and herbs. **Louisiana State Archives Building,** 3851 Essen, contains changing exhibits on Louisiana history, including original documents, newspapers, letters, etc. Open weekdays, 8-4:30.

Southern University, Harding Boulevard, founded in 1880, flagship campus of the Southern University system, one of the largest, predominantly black universities in the country, sits on a bluff overlooking a bend in the Mississippi River. Attractions include "Red Stick" monument sculpture, president's home, Clark Activity Center, the Black Heritage Exhibit Series in the library, the Student Union Art Gallery, and the caged mascot, LaCumba, a jaguar. For SU campus information on sporting events, special exhibits, and performances, call (504-771-4500). **Cohn Memorial Arboretum,** Foster Road, is a 16-acre tract of hilly terrain planted with over 250 species of native and introduced trees and shrubs. Paved walks. Open weekdays, 8-5; weekends, 9-5. (504-775-1006). **Greater Baton Rouge Zoo,** Thomas Road, features over 900 animals in spacious, natural habitat settings. Programs. Open daily, 10-5; summer weekends, 10-6. Admission. (504-775-3877). **Festforall,** third weekend in May, held outdoors and in downtown Baton Rouge facilities, includes visual and performing arts, children's activities, entertainment, food. **River Cities Blues Festival,** second weekend in April, downtown, features Baton Rouge blues and other live music on several stages. Food. **Fall Crafts Festival,** third weekend in October, is a juried show of craftsmen from all over the country. Food.

BAKER: On La. 19, in a restored Victorian cottage built in 1906, is the **Heritage Museum** and cultural center featuring artifacts and memorabilia related to turn-of-the-century rural lifestyle. Ten outbuildings on the grounds. Open Mon.-Fri., 10-4; weekends, 1-4. Admission. (504-774-1776)

ZACHARY: McHugh House Museum, 4524 Virginia, is a restored Victorian home built in 1903, furnished to recreate the original period with clothing and artifacts from early 1900s to 1950. Open daily, 9-12 and by appt. Donations. (504-654-1912)

FALSE RIVER AREA: False River is a picturesque oxbow lake, formed when the Mississippi River changed its course. A marker at the north end marks its cutoff from the Mississippi. Offers fishing, boating, skiing. Numerous plantation homes are in the area and worth a visit or drive-by. Highways 413, 414, 415, and 416 can be followed to make the complete loop of the area. At Glynn, La. 416 south, is the site of **Glynnwood Plantation,** a large, rambling cottage begun in 1836, enlarged in 1875, and again in 1890 to effect the Victorian-style appearance. Open by appt. Admission. (504-627-4194 or 627-5641). **Alma Plantation**, circa 1789, is among the area's last few working sugar mills. Drive-by. **Maison Chenal** on Highway 414 is a late-18th-century home built by Julien Poydras surrounded by late-18th-century-style landscape. By appt. Admission. (504-627-5860). **LeBeau House** on Highway 414 was built in 1840 overlooking Chenal Bayou. The house and kitchen are on the National Register. By appt. to groups. Admission. (504-638-4468). **Parlange Plantation,** La. 1 overlooking False River, is an 18th-century house furnished with family heirlooms. Open daily except holidays, 9-5. Admission. (504-638-8410). (See essay). **Pleasantview,** built in the early 19th century, is a Creole raised cottage overlooking False River and surrounded by 10 acres of gardens. Open by appt. Admission. (504-627-4662). **The Fall Pilgrimage,** 4th weekend in October, features tours of plantation homes, gardens, and other area attractions. Admission.

NEW ROADS: the town was one of the first settlements after the Louisiana Purchase, attracting trappers, then planters of tobacco and sugarcane to the area. New Roads is dotted with small cottages and plantation homes dating from the mid-to late 19th century. **Pointe Coupee Museum and Tourist Center,** La. 1 on False River, is a small, piece-sur-piece style cottage with bousillage walls, restored and furnished with early Louisiana artifacts. The Tourist Center offers information, maps, brochures of the area. Open Tues.-Sat., 10-3. (504-638-9858). **Pointe Coupee Chamber of Commerce,** Courthouse Annex, downtown, also has information, maps, and brochures. (504-638-3500). **Pointe Coupee Parish Courthouse,** Main, was built in 1902, featuring Romanesque Revival exterior with turrets and square tower. **St. Francis Chapel,** Pointe Coupee Road, dates to 1738. The Victorian

Gothic building was moved to the present location in 1895 and rebuilt. A 200-year-old cypress statue carved by Indians remains; the chapel bell, from 1760, was salvaged from a shipwreck on the river. By appt. (504-638-8165). **Bonnie Glen,** La. 1, is a raised plantation in Creole-Greek Revival style. The 200-year-old barn is of interest. By appt. Admission. (504-638-9004). **Wycliffe** on Highway 415 west of New Roads was built circa 1820, the site of a now-disappeared community. By appt. Admission. (504-638-9504). **Mardi Gras,** celebrated in New Roads on Fat Tuesday, with morning and afternoon parades, floats, costumes, food.

ORANGE GROVE STORE: La. 415, 11 miles north of U.S. 190, is an antebellum plantation commissary that once served Orange Grove Plantation, now a museum with store furnishings. Open Fri., Sat., Sun., by appt. Admission. (504-344-4406)

ROSEDALE: off La. 77, **Episcopal Church of the Nativity,** a cypress church built in 1859 surrounded by 3 enormous live oaks. **Live Oaks Plantation,** La. 77, built in 1838, includes the 2-story cypress, galleried main house, and several vintage outbuildings. By appt. Admission. (504-648-2346)

SHERBURNE WILDLIFE MANAGEMENT AREA: off U.S. 190 west near Krotz Springs, is a 27,000-acre wilderness, tangent to Big Alabama Bayou, offering primitive camping, fishing, hunting, boat launch.

ERWINVILLE: site of the State Capitol Dragway, U.S. 190 west, featuring scheduled drag racing events including the Cajun Nationals. (504-928-7772)

PORT ALLEN: La. 1, west of the Mississippi River, is the location of the Port of Baton Rouge, 4th largest American seaport by tonnage and the most inland deepwater port in the country, where river barges exchange goods with oceangoing vessels. (504-387-4207). **West Baton Rouge Tourist Commission** has information, maps, and brochures of the area. 2800 Frontage Road, just before the Mississippi River bridge entrance. (504-344-2927). **The West Baton Rouge Parish Museum,** 845 N. Jefferson, housed in the old West Baton Rouge Parish neoclassical courthouse, contains an interesting collection of historical items and period pieces from the area dating from the 19th century, an American Empire-style bedroom, changing exhibits. On the grounds is the Aillet House, circa 1830, a French Creole cottage. Open Tues.-Sat., 10-4:30; Sun., 2-5. (504-583-2392). **St. John the Baptist Catholic Church,** built in 1907, is a wood-frame church still in use. **Allendale Plantation,** U.S. 190 west, built in 1852 by Gov. Henry Watkins Allen, and **Poplar Grove Plantation**, built as the Banker's Pavilion for the

1884 World's Cotton and Industrial Exposition in New Orleans, now on La. 1 north, are drive-bys. Plantation Lights at Poplar Grove, mid-to late December, featuring 1/2-mile drive through Christmas-lit cabins and sugar mill, other activities. Admission. **Catherine Plantation,** U.S. 190 west, drive-by. **Cinclare Plantation,** La. 1 south near Brusly, one of the South's oldest sugar mills, is still in use. Drive-by. **Port Allen Locks,** off La. 1 south, are working locks that allow passage of large boats and tows from the Intracoastal Waterway to the Mississippi River. Visitors welcome daily, 9-4.

BRUSLY: (pronounced brew-ly) The Back Brusly Oak is a member of the Louisiana Live Oak Society and estimated to be over 350 years old. **Drive-bys:** Lockman House; Antonio House, La. 1 north, built circa 1800; and Cazenave House, La. 1, built circa 1835. **St. John the Baptist Cemetery** near the St. John the Baptist Catholic Church dates from the mid-1830s.

PLAQUEMINE: this area along the Mississippi River and west to the Atchafalaya Basin is one of the first Acadian coasts in Louisiana. **Plaquemine City Hall,** Main at Church, built in 1849 to serve as the Iberville Parish Courthouse, is a Greek Revival structure. The **Plaquemine Locks** were completed in 1909 to connect the navigable Bayou Plaquemine with the Mississippi River. At the time of their construction, they had the highest freshwater lift in the world. Now a visitors complex in the original lockhouse exhibits on the theme of river traffic and trade and water craft used in the area. Picnic grounds and observation tower. Open daily. Plaquemine Lockhouse on the grounds offers information from Iberville Parish Tourist Commission (504-687-0641). **International Acadian Festival,** celebrating the Acadians' arrival in Louisiana, is held the 3rd weekend in October at the Plaquemine Locks. Arts and crafts, entertainment, heritage, food. (504-687-7319). St. Basil's Academy, built circa 1850, was the site of a convent and Catholic school for over 115 years. **Middleton Home,** built on a Spanish land grant before 1842, is Louisiana classical style. Drive-by. **St. Louis Plantation,** River Road, is a Greek Revival-style home built in 1858 of cypress on a location known as Home Plantation when established in 1807. Open May 1-Nov. 15, except Sun., 9-5. Admission. **Variety Plantation**, Bayou Road, is a Greek Revival-style cottage built in 1850 with dependency buildings. By appt. (504-659-2510). **Live Oaks Plantation,** Bayou Grosse Tete, is the oldest plantation home in the parish, with a main house, gardens, and slave church. Drive-by. **Old Turnerville,** north La. 1, features two restored and furnished 19th-century homes. Open Mon.-Sat., 10-4; Sun., 1-4. Admission. (504-687-5337)

ATCHAFALAYA SWAMP: Atchafalaya means "long river" in Attakapas language. This is Louisiana's most famous and North America's largest river-basin swamp. The Atchafalaya River runs from the Old River Control Structure to Atchafalaya Bay. The width of the swamp is maintained by protection levees. The area is a virtual paradise for scenery, hunting, and fishing. Access to the east side of the swamp is available past Plaquemine, off La. 75, at public boat launches at Bayou Sorrel and Bayou Pigeon.

BAYOU GOULA: on La. 405 between Point Pleasant and Bayou Goula is the **Chapel of the Madonna,** built in 1890 and known as the "smallest church in the world." It fulfills a pledge by a devout Italian woman for her daughter's recovery from serious illness. Annual mass on August 15. **Tally-Ho,** La. 405, was the overseer's home, taken over by the owners of the plantation when the main house burned. Drive-by.

NOTTOWAY: La. 405 at White Castle, completed in 1859, is the largest plantation home in the South. With 64 rooms, restored to its glory of a blend of Greek Revival and Italianate styles, it is often called the White Castle. On River Road, surrounded by spacious, oak-shaded grounds, open daily, 9-5. Closed Christmas. Admission. (504-545-2730)

DONALDSONVILLE: founded in 1750, is the 3rd oldest town in Louisiana, settled after Natchitoches in 1714 and New Orleans in 1718. Located at the intersection of Bayou Lafourche and the Mississippi River, the town began as a trading post. Its downtown area is a National Register Historic District with buildings from 1865 through the 1930s. Louisiana Square, a mid-city park, was designated on the original city plan and laid out in 1806. Local tourist information available from the Chamber of Commerce (504-473-4814). **Old Courthouse/Jail,** built in 1865-69, is now the Ascension Heritage Association Museum exhibiting vintage architectural tools and displays depicting the architectural styles of the town. Open weekends, 9-4. **Ascension Catholic Church,** completed in 1896, features massive imported marble columns. The church parish was established in 1772 by order of Charles III of Spain. **St. Vincent's Institute,** circa 1850, was originally the Daughters of Charity Convent and is now used as a school. **St. Peter's Methodist Church,** built in 1871, is still in use. **B. Lemann & Brothers, Inc.,** Mississippi Street at Railroad Avenue, was built in 1836 in the Italianate commercial style and is the oldest department store building in Louisiana. **Sunshine Bridge,** built during the administration of the "Singing Governor," Jimmie Davis, crosses the Mississippi River from Donaldsonville to Burnside. **Mardi Gras,**

Cypress trees in the Atchafalaya Swamp. (Photograph by Mary Ann Sternberg)

celebrated on Fat Tuesday, with a parade of floats and antique vehicles. **St. Emma Plantation,** La. 1 south, is a Greek Revival house built in 1850, the site of a Civil War skirmish in 1862. Drive-by. **Sunshine Festival and Great River Road Rally,** in October, includes a rally-sprint classic car show, fireworks, carnival, arts and crafts, and entertainment.

Unique Louisiana

PARLANGE

Louisiana is rich with plantation homes that reflect its cultural cross-currents, from ornate and extravagant columned stereotypes of the antebellum south to modest cottages hidden behind comfortable galleries and tucked under high-pitched tin roofs. The luckiest houses have been impeccably maintained or restored by loving owners; less fortunate ones are merely sustained. The saddest are those that have already vanished, ravaged by time or victimized by disinterest.

Parlange is unique among Louisiana plantations. More than a survivor, it sits pristinely amid towering, moss-draped oaks, cosseted by small gardens, overlooking the shimmering waters of False River. Graceful and elegant, it is one of the few remaining gems of French Colonial architecture, beautifully crafted of native materials — handmade brick, cypress, and bousillage (mud, moss, and deer hair) walls over-plastered. The site has earned a secure place in history, through its longevity as well as its significance — the encampment of Union Army troops on its front lawn, and visits by both Confederate and Union generals.

So Parlange would deserve veneration for its site and style, as well as a footnote to area Civil War lore. But another added distinction makes it unique: since 1750, when Marquis Vincent de Ternant built the house on a land grant from the French Crown, Parlange has belonged to and remained in the same family — over two hundred years of a continuous line of heirship. Named for Charles Parlange, second husband of Madame Ternant, the property has been passed to successive generations of Parlanges who, in turn, have lived in, used, and served the plantation for all of its existence.

At many vintage homes, interiors are furnished "of the period"; sometimes, a few of the pieces may even be "original to the house." At Parlange, furnishings are not only "of the period," but "original to the family." The only questions are "what period" and "which family member?" The furniture, decorative accessories, artifacts, and personal memorabilia are the massed acquisition of generations, reflecting not only the long thread of family history but also the taste of

122

individuals. Characteristically, the family portrait gallery is a collection containing eighteenth-century oil miniatures and contemporary color snapshots, all displayed with equality on the polished patina of an antique chest.

Museum houses are for visitors; Parlange is a home for the family who lives there. Visitors merely come, by appointment, to view a lived-in house, the centerpiece of a still-working plantation. Yet, they find an almost palpable sense of history, layers of tradition so vivid as to be nearly visible. There are no ghosts at Parlange, but rather an accumulated soul. It makes the plantation more than a physical place. It is the ultimate Family Home.

Houma/Thibodaux Area

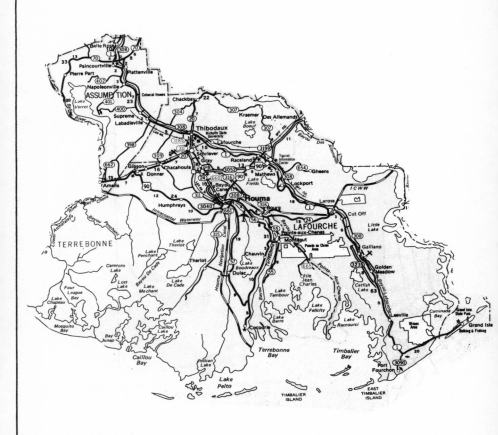

7

Houma/Thibodaux and the South Central

Bayou Lafourche (pronounced "la-foosh") has defined life in this area since the arrival of the first settlers. Bayou Lafourche meanders through flat terrain from Donaldsonville to the gulf, followed on the high ground of its west bank by La. Highway 1, called "the longest street in the world" and an interesting drive. The bayou was a tributary of the Mississippi River until the levee system was built, reducing it to a flat, still channel. A pumping plant constructed at Donaldsonville remedied the situation.

The land is dotted with lovely old plantation homes; industries loom over the landscape casting geometric shadows across sweeps of cane field. Acadians settled the area, farming narrow strips of land, hunting, fishing, and trapping to provide for their families. These are still important economic and recreational activities and, with the oil service and marine service industries, have contributed as much to the local culture as to the economy.

Assumption, Lafourche, and Terrebonne parishes comprise this area where Houma is the largest city.

PAINCOURTVILLE: (pronounced "panker-vill"), on La. 403, is the location of **St. Elizabeth Church,** built in 1890, featuring frescoes created by an exiled Mexican priest which show the Church battling various forms of heresy. **Dugas & Leblanc Sugar Mill,** La. 1, offers tours of sugarcane processing in season. By appt. (504-369-6450)

PIERRE PART: La. 70, west of La. 1, is the site of Virgin's Island in tiny Bayou Pierre Part. A statue of the Virgin Mary was placed there by residents who saved it from a flood in 1882 that destroyed the church and many homes. The island was dedicated to the Virgin in the hopes that she would intercede to prevent future occurrences. **Camp Bayou**

Corne, La. 70 west, is a recreation area used by residents since the days of only buggy and pirogue transportation. Camping, fishing, boat launch.

PLATTENVILLE: on La. 308, the **Church of the Assumption** is a Gothic Revival church built in 1856 on the site of the first church ever built on Bayou Lafourche.

NAPOLEONVILLE: La. 1, **Christ Episcopal Church,** Main Street, built in 1853 in the Gothic style, was dedicated by Leonidas Polk, the "Fighting Bishop." Union troops stabled their horses in the church during the Civil War. The cemetery behind the church features neo-classical funerary. **Madewood Plantation,** La. 308 south, on Bayou Lafourche, was built in 1846 and is considered one of the finest examples of Greek Revival architecture in the South. Restored and furnished with antiques of the period, with the original kitchen, carriage house, and cemetery on the property, the complex is open daily, except holidays, 10-5. Admission. (504-369-7151). **Christmas Heritage Banquet,** second Saturday in December, features a Victorian Christmas celebration with dining and entertainment. Admission.

SUPREME: the Supreme Sugar Refinery, La. 1, offers tours in grinding season by appt. (504-369-6796)

LAKE VERRET: between La. 1 and 70 in the Atchafalaya Basin, the lake is a popular local fishing spot. Boat launch.

KRAEMER: several tours of the swamp leave from this town.

DES ALLEMANDS: literally, "the Germans" in French, U.S. 90, was settled by German immigrants over 250 years ago, as were several other towns in this area known as the German Coast. **Louisiana Catfish Festival,** held the second weekend in July, features championship road race, catfish skinning contest, beauty pageant, entertainment, and food. (504-758-7542)

SALVADOR WILDLIFE MANAGEMENT AREA: located along the northwest shore of Lake Salvador, this 31,000-acre, primarily freshwater marsh tract is accessible by boat and offers hunting, trapping by permit, excellent fishing, nature study, boating, and picnicking. (504-568-5885)

EDWARD DOUGLASS WHITE HOME SITE: La. 1, 5 miles north of Thibodaux, is a raised cottage of handhewn, pegged cypress built in 1790 that was the home of Edward Douglass White, judge, governor of Louisiana, and U.S. senator. It was also the birthplace of his son, Edward Douglass White, Jr., who served on the Louisiana Supreme Court, the U.S. Senate, and as both associate justice and chief justice of the U.S. Supreme Court. Drive-by.

THIBODAUX: founded in 1820 on the site of the first trading post established between New Orleans and the Teche country. **Thibodaux Chamber of Commerce,** 100 Green, offers information, maps, and brochures. (504-446-1187). **St. Joseph Co-Cathedral,** 7th Street, a replica of a Parisian cathedral, has vaulted ceiling, ornate frescoes, stained-glass windows, and a brilliant rose window above the choir loft. **St. John's Episcopal Church,** Jackson at 7th, built in 1844 by Leonidas Polk, is the oldest Episcopal church west of the Mississippi River. Its vestibule and slave gallery, now a choir loft, were added in 1856. The gravesite of Francis Nicholls is in the cemetery. **Lafourche Parish Courthouse,** Green Street, completed in 1860, one of the best preserved old public buildings, is in the classical style with a copper domed roof. **Jean Lafitte National Park, Wetlands Culture Center**, St. Mary Highway, features exhibits and interpretive program about bayou Cajun life. Open daily except holidays. (504-448-1375). **Nicholls State University,** La. 1, founded in 1948 on a 166-acre campus includes: *Allen J. Ellender Room,* first floor of Ellender Memorial Library, displays cultural and historical displays of southwest Louisiana. The Archives and Special Collections houses the personal records and artifacts of U.S. Senator Ellender as well as an oral history collection. *Center for Traditional Boat Building,* first floor of Ellender Library, is open for visitors to see the traditional folk boats being constructed. Weekdays, 8-4:30 during semesters. *Historical Research Center* contains Catholic church records dating back to 1817, historical material, and art. For campus information on special performances, exhibits, and events, call (504-446-8111).

    Martha Sowell Utley Memorial Library and Cultural Center, La. 1, a renovated early-20th-century warehouse featuring a monumental false front of Italianate design, houses the main branch of the Lafourche Parish Library, the Thibodaux Playhouse, and an art gallery. (504-447-4119). Numerous private plantation homes in the Thibodaux area are worth seeing as drive-bys, including **Rienzi,** on La. 308, built in 1796 with Spanish-style double stairways, and **Acadia,** La. 1 just south of Nicholls State, built in 1828 by Jim Bowie, and many others. **Fireman's Fair,** held the third weekend in April, features a parade that has marched since 1857, carnival rides, auctions, music, and food. **Mardi Gras** is celebrated with parades two weekends before Fat Tuesday and several parades on Mardi Gras day. **Laurel Valley Plantation Village,** La. 308, 2 miles south of Thibodaux, is the largest intact, turn-of-the-century sugar plantation complex in the south. Rows of tenant houses stretch down a cane-lined drive. More than 70 buildings remain. Tours by appt. Admission. **The Laurel Valley Village General Store** is open Tues.-Sun., 10-4. (504-446-7456). Three Cajun festivals are held at Laurel Valley annually featuring crafts, Cajun food, and performances.

GIBSON: Wildlife Gardens, off U.S. 90, features a unique native Louisiana wildlife exhibit including alligators, birds, ducks, deer, and other swamp habitat flora and fauna. Tours Mon.-Sat., at 10, 1, 3:30. Admission. (504-575-3676). **Swamp tours of the Chacahoula Swamp** and other Atchafalaya Basin outings leave from here. Boat rentals.

RACELAND: at the junction of U.S. 90 and La. 1 is the **Lafourche Parish Tourist Office,** housed in a renovated fire station, offering information, maps, and brochures. Open weekdays, 9-4. (504-537-5800). In the same facility is a small museum exhibit of stuffed area wildlife, local paintings, and crafts. **St. Mary's Nativity Church,** on La. 1, built in 1850, has an old cemetery with above-ground tombs. **South Coast Sugar Refinery,** La. 3199, offers tours during grinding season, Oct.-Dec., by appt. (504-537-3533). **Sauce Piquante Festival,** on the St. Mary's Church grounds, held the first weekend in October, features pirogue races, art, decoy carvers, children's entertainment, and food. (504-537-7544). **Rosella,** built in 1814, is a fine example of a raised cottage in the French Normandy style, restored and open by appt. (504-537-5800)

MATHEWS: La Vie LaFourchaise Festival, held the third weekend in October, celebrates the lifestyle, heritage, and culture of Lafourche Parish as it was a century ago, including priests arriving by pirogue, period costumes, open-air mass, music, antique syrup mill, soap making, blacksmith, boucherie. (504-537-5800)

LOCKPORT: La. 308, Bollinger's Shipyard offers tours through the facility where Coast Guard patrol boats are built. By appt. (504-532-2512)

HOUMA: the parish seat of Terrebonne (meaning "good earth") Parish is named for the Houmas Indian tribe and was settled in 1834. Seven bayous, the Houma navigation canal, and the Intracoastal Waterway converge in the town, earning it the nickname, "Venice of America." Numerous bridges link the banks of the waterways that traverse the town that was formerly the center of the area's offshore oil industry. **The Houma/Terrebonne Tourist Commission,** U.S. 90 at S. St. Charles Street, offers information, maps, brochures, walking and driving guides, and swamp tour literature. (504-868-2732). **Houma-Terrebonne Arts and Humanities Council** offers information on special exhibits, performances, and events. (504-872-6975). **The Houma National Register Historic District** includes a variety of residential architectural styles, including Creole, shotgun, and Victorian. **St. Matthew's Church,** 243 Barrow, built in 1892 of local cypress in the carpenter Gothic style with stained-glass windows, replaces a brick structure on the site built in 1859. By appt. (504-868-2732). **St. Francis de Sales Cathedral,** 300 Verret, is Gothic revival brick structure built in 1938 replacing the original church, dedicated in 1847, which was destroyed by the great hurricane of 1926. A plaza and fountain in front relate to the area's French-Spanish heritage. The cemetery, begun in the mid-19th century, includes above-ground crypts and French inscriptions.

Terrebonne Parish Courthouse, built in 1937, is an art-deco structure replacing an earlier Romanesque courthouse with clock tower. The Courthouse Square is pre-Civil War and its oak trees are on the National Live Oak Register. **Southdown Plantation House and Terrebonne Museum,** La. 311 at St. Charles, built in 1859 in the Greek Revival style, was added to in 1893, changing the architecture to Queen Anne Victorian. The Minors, who owned the plantation, are credited with propagating in the 1920s a variety of sugarcane resistant to mosaic disease, saving Louisiana's sugar industry. The museum displays Boehm and Doughty porcelain birds, a recreation of U.S. Sen. Allen Ellender's Washington office, original bedroom furniture of the Minor family, and a collection of Terrebonnne Parish oral history. Open daily except holidays, 10-4. Admission. (504-851-0154). **The Southdown Marketplace,** exhibiting arts and crafts in a festival atmosphere, is held the first Saturday in November and the Saturday before Easter weekend on the lawn of Southdown. **Ardoyne Plantation,** La. 311 north of Houma, built in 1897 in the Victorian Gothic style, is modeled after a Scottish castle. By appt. (504-872-3197). **Magnolia Plantation,** La. 311 north (near the town of Schriever), built in 1858, is a cypress mansion that served as a temporary hospital during local Civil War skirmishes. By appt. Admission. (504-446-1493). **Bayou Drive** is a circular driving tour that follows several bayous and offers views of picturesque scenery, shrimp and oyster boats, and other local color.

Grand Bois Park, La. 24 east of La. 55, is a 50-acre park known for its large stand of woods, good for bird-watching. Camping. (504-594-7410). **Hercules Den**, La. 57 south, offers a tour of the Carnival krewe's Mardi Gras costumes, floats, and props. By appt. Admission. (504-872-0444) **Mardi Gras** features two weekends of parades, culminating on Fat Tuesday with three parades. **Houma-Terrebonne Christmas Festival,** held the first Saturday in December, features a parade, football bowl, arts and crafts, and entertainment. **Louisiana Praline Festival,** held the first weekend in May, features the world's largest praline, praline cooking contests, food, woodcarvers, music tents.

Swamp tours abound in the Houma area, as well as charter fishing boats and bird-watching. Inquire.

CHAUVIN: The Blessing of the Fleet is held the third Sunday of April, at the opening of the shrimping season, to bless all boats for a prosperous season. Contest for the best decorated boats. (504-594-5859). **Boudreaux Canal General Store**, off La. 56, is a 50-year-old general store. Open weekdays, 7:30-4; Sat., 7:30-noon. **Seafood packing plant tours,** showing the process of seafood marketing from unloading to freezing, by appt. (504-868-2732). **Lagniappe on the Bayou,** held the second weekend in October, features food, fais-do-do, dancing, crafts, costumes. Camping space. (504-594-5859). **La Trouvaille,** entertainment and meal illuminating the daily lifestyle of the Cajuns, Oct.-May. Admission. (504-873-8005)

DULAC: Houmas Indian Center, in the Dulac Community Center, is the tribal home of the Houmas Indians. (504-563-7483). **Blessing of the Shrimp Fleet**, April, features decorated boats in a parade and religious ceremony.

COCODRIE: near the end of La. 56. Numerous charter boats, fishing and hunting guides operate out of this small fishing village. **LUMCON,** the Louisiana Universities Marine Center, houses labs, classrooms, offices, and research facility in a building elevated to withstand hurricanes in the marsh. The public exhibit area features aquaria displaying a range of the environments of coastal Louisiana and an observation platform. By appt. (504-851-2800)

LAROSE: is located at the intersection of La. 1 and the Intracoastal Waterway, and by Bayou Lafourche—a boat-watcher's paradise. The French Food Festival takes place the last weekend in October.

CUT OFF: a picturesque fishing town that offers a perspective on life along the bayou and hosts several local cultural festivals, including La Fete du Bayou, last weekend in September.

POINTE AU CHIEN WILDLIFE MANAGEMENT AREA: off La. 1, south of Cut Off, is a marshland tract of 29,000 acres ranging from nearly fresh to brackish. Access to the interior is by boat. Hunting, fishing, crabbing, shrimping, boating, nature study, and bird-watching. (504-568-5885)

GALLIANO: La. 308. The Cajun Heritage Festival, held the third weekend in August, features competition and displays of wooden duck carvings, miniature boat building, food, and entertainment. (504-632-4633). **Bayou Christmas**, held the second weekend in December, features a parade of decorated boats along Bayou Lafourche.

GOLDEN MEADOW: La. 1, named for the vast fields of goldenrod that surrounded it and which covered the "black gold" and natural gas discovered in 1938. **Petit Caporal,** a quaint, old shrimp boat built in 1854, the oldest existing boat of its kind in the state, is on display on the bank of Bayou Lafourche in the center of town commemorating the area's important shrimping industry. The Blessing of the Fleet takes place each year on the first weekend in August, since 1916. **Seafood processing tour** available by appt. (504-537-5800)

PORT FOURCHON-FOURCHON CITY: off La. 1 south on La. 3090, where Bayou Lafourche meets the Gulf of Mexico, is a harbor for deep sea fishing charter boats and an industrial base for offshore oil drilling. This is a prime bird-watching area. Public beach, fishing, crabbing, and primitive camping. **Louisiana Offshore Oil Port (LOOP),** the nation's only superport—a deepwater pumping terminal for supertankers—is located in the Gulf of Mexico.

WISNER WILDLIFE MANAGEMENT AREA: off La. 1, the 21,000-acre salt marsh is accessible by boat, offering hunting, fishing, crabbing, shrimping, boating, bird-watching. Public launch available along La. 1, which splits the tract. (504-568-5612)

GRAND ISLE: on the Gulf of Mexico, at the end of La. 1, is actually located in Jefferson Parish. It is Louisiana's gulf coast resort, with sand beaches, picnicking, fishing, crabbing, camping, and launch ramps. Fishing charters. Public fishing on the old highway bridge. **Grand Isle East State Park,** on the east end of La. 1, is a 140-acre site with a 400-foot fishing pier that offers day and night fishing. Swimming, primitive camping. Admission. (504-787-2559). **International Grand Isle Tarpon Rodeo,** the oldest competitive fishing contest in the country, is held the third week in July. The Louisiana Department of Wildlife and Fisheries labels and displays each catch. Fee to enter. **Grand Isle tour** features sightseeing of Grand Isle and a visit to Grand Terre Island by converted shrimp boat. Admission. (504-787-3744 and 787-3179)

GRAND TERRE ISLAND: east of Grand Isle, accessible by boat only. **Fort Livingston** is a large masonry fort facing Grand Isle on the west side, built by the U.S. Army from 1835 to 1861. Explore on foot. **The Lyle S. St. Amant Marine Laboratory,** an experimental station of the Louisiana Department of Wildlife and Fisheries, is open weekdays to visitors and features exhibits of marine life.

Unique Louisiana

HOW TO BUILD A PIROGUE

The pirogue (pronounced *pee-ro,* or *pee-rog*), Louisiana's best-known, small, native boat, is narrow, flat-bottomed, and pointed on both ends, the perfect craft for poling or paddling shallow bayous and rivers, or for travelling deep into the swamp and marshlands to hunt and fish. Backwoods Cajuns swear it can travel on dew.

The word "pirogue" is derived from a French or Spanish interpretation of the Carib Indian word for "dugout" because the crafts were traditionally made from hollowing out a large cypress log. French settlers in south Louisiana adapted the Indians' styling, and with their more sophisticated tools, were able to make a lighter, stabler boat— easier to paddle and portage.

But by the end of the 1930s and Louisiana's great logging period, few cypress logs large enough to make dugouts were left, forcing Cajun boatbuilders to substitute cypress planking and to fabricate, rather than dig out, a trusty craft. Today, with the increasing cost of cypress, boatbuilders even substitute marine plywood in the shell, though insisting that the essential structural elements of the pirogue must still be cypress. Despite the change in materials, however, the shape and use of pirogues is much the same as it was 250 years ago, when the first Acadian settlers planted themselves in south Louisiana.

In Pierre Part, the heart of Cajun country, pirogues are still important for crawfishing, fishing, and trapping, so the fine art of building a pirogue lives on. One skillful pirogue-maker takes about three working days to build a standard-size, twelve-foot boat, carefully cutting and fitting the elements to ensure a leakproof product. But he never tests his finished product for seaworthiness. "I garontee it's gonna be watertight. . . . No water's gonna get in 'less you fall overboard and get back in wet!" He's been in the business far too long to be stretching the truth.

This is how he says to build a pirogue:

First, saw two headblocks—one for the bow, one for the stern. These elongated pyramids are always made of cypress, and their size and shape, as well as the pitch of the center angle, determine the length and width of the boat.

From the long sides of a sheet of four-foot, 3/8" marine plywood, cut two slightly curved boards for gunwales. The height of the boards is 10 3/4" on each end, curving to 12" in the middle—"like the rocker on a rocking chair." The top edge of the gunwale is straight cut. Cutting off the gunwales leaves a piece of plywood shaped like a fat hourglass—a perfectly fitted floorboard.

The two gunwales are nailed to the headblocks, creating a fat, canoe shape. To reduce the width, attach a jig—a homemade wooden pattern wider at the top than the bottom—to the sides with C-clamps. How far up on the jig the gunwales are clamped determines the width of the pirogue. For easier manipulating, the stern is always slightly narrower than the bow.

Then the cypress ribs and uprights (floor joints and gunwale supports) are nailed in. The ribs run straight across the floor, nailed to the blocky, spatula-shaped uprights. The uprights are nailed to the interior of the gunwales. There are five ribs and five pairs of uprights in a twelve-foot pirogue.

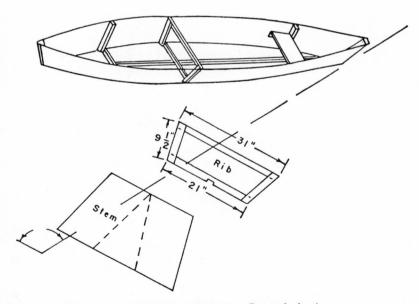

(Courtesy Louisiana Wildlife and Fisheries Commission)

Next fit are the nose pieces—decorative triangular wedges behind each headblock, drilled for a rope hole. To the front of the headblocks are added finishing headblocks—specially shaped wooden strips that even out the extreme bow and stern exteriors.

Nail cypress bumper rails on the top and bottom of the outside of the gunwale. (The bottom rail is necessary only when marine plywood is used because the floorboard can't be directly nailed into the end of a piece of plywood without splitting it.)

Flip the boat over and plane the bottom surfaces smooth before nailing on the floorboard. First nail the ribs, then nail the railing all the way around. Quick-drying glue is applied at the same time the elements are nailed in place, to seal any potential leaks.

This highly regarded boatbuilder doesn't varnish or paint his finished craft. "I jes' do the woodwork, me," he grins, recommending that the buyer add a finishing coat to prolong the life of his pirogue before he drops it in the bayou . . . or sets out across the dew.

8

The Greater
New Orleans Area

New Orleans, queen city of Louisiana and one of the most interesting cities in the United States, is called by natives *New Or-luns,* or *New Aw-yuns,* or *N'Awlins,* but never *New Or-leens*—except in the lyrics "d'ya know what it means/to miss . . . ?" The city was founded in 1718 by Bienville, who established a tiny French colony in a sharp bend of the Mississippi River on high ground the Indians had already recognized. The French Quarter was established on that site. New Orleans'colorful history is woven through French and Spanish rule, the arrival of Americans after the Louisiana Purchase, important battles in the War of 1812 and the Civil War, and the progress of the 20th century with an accelerated pace of commerce and the oil industry. But if dates, places, and names are the benchmarks in New Orleans history, the tangible details of who and what and how are also the dashes and splashes that have contributed to the creation of a uniquely rich culture.

The metropolitan area, which encompasses at least parts of four parishes, is composed of a variety of historic districts, suburbs, and ex-urbs. Beyond the city to the north, on the north shore of Lake Pontchartrain, are small towns, many of which developed in the ozone belt as summer resorts for the well-to-do of the Crescent City or along railroad lines. North of them are Louisiana's eastern Florida Parishes, scenic, wooded, hilly, and primarily rural. To the south of New Orleans, the swamp and marsh that Bienville noted intrude quickly; the largest communities are strung along waterways that were once the only highways. It is flat, low, and wild down to the gulf, with a sprinkling of Cajun influence as well as that of other cultures of peoples who set down their roots beyond the cosmopolitan center.

New Orleans Area

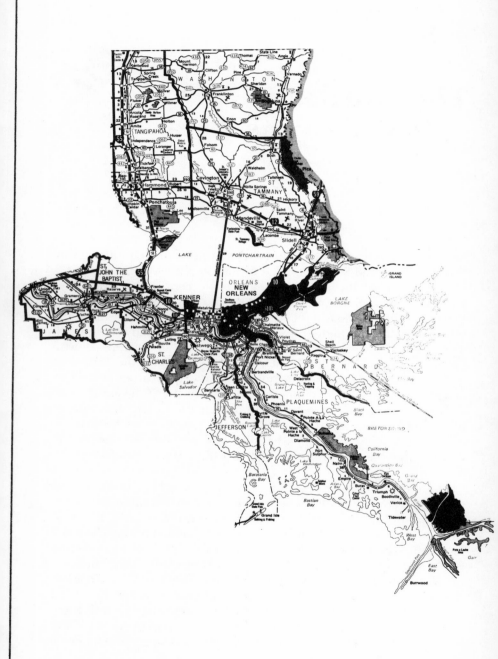

Washington, Tangipahoa, St. Tammany, Orleans, Jefferson, St. Bernard, Plaquemines, St. Charles, St. John the Baptist, and St. James are the parishes that comprise this region.

WASHINGTON PARISH: in the northeast corner of the "toe" of Louisiana's boot, is a hilly, primarily rural area, settled late, where small farming and a significant timber industry that began at the turn of the century are significant. **Bogalusa:** La. 10, in the heart of the yellow pine belt. The Bogue Lusa (means black creek) runs through the town. **The Bogalusa Chamber of Commerce** offers information on area attractions and events. (504-735-5731). **Bogalusa City Hall,** 202 Arkansas, built in 1917, is handsome example of rural Renaissance Revival architecture, constructed entirely of long-leaf yellow pine. **Sullivan House,** 223 S. Border, built in 1907, was constructed by William Sullivan, known as "the father of Bogalusa," in a combination of Queen Anne and classical revival styles. It is located in a section of town called Little Buffalo, because so many lumber company officials came from Buffalo, New York. **Bogalusa Railroad Station,** built in 1907, is a classic turn-of-the-century rural depot, no longer in use. **Cassidy Park** is a midtown public, city park with petting zoo, recreational facilities, and two museums. The *Lousiana Museum of Indian Culture,* features artifacts of the state's Indian tribes. Open weekends or by appt. (504-732-4008). *Bogue Lusa Pioneer Museum* houses a large collection of antique tools and artifacts. Open Sat., 10-4; Sun., 1-4. (504-732-4238). **Lake Vista Nature Preserve Trail,** 10 miles east of Bogalusa, is a 1-mile hiking trail through pine woods and cypress swamp area.

Franklinton: Franklinton Chamber of Commerce offers information on area attractions and events. (504-839-5080). **Robert Babington House,** 608 Main, built in 1906 in Queen Anne style, is the most elaborate residence in the area. Private; drive-by. **Mile Branch Settlement** is a replica village depicting pioneer life in the area in the late 19th century, including homes, post office, general store, syrup mill, blacksmith, church, and furnishings and artifacts of the period. The Knight Cabin, a small log cabin built in 1857, and Sylvest House, a late example of a log dogtrot built about 1880, are two important attractions. Tours of Mile Branch Village are by appt. or during the Washington Parish Fair. Admission. (504-839-6485). **The Washington Parish Fair,** established in 1910, held in mid-October, features Mile Branch Village, livestock show, country market, carnival, entertainment, folklife crafts exhibitions, food. (504-839-5822). **Frickie's Cave,** La. 25, 6 miles south of Franklinton, is a 47-acre area, an eroded pit in the rolling hills that has formed a steep canyon and red clay domes.

Walking. **Old Choctaw Trail,** marker on La. 10 east, was a trail cut by the Choctaw for trade with Indians in Baton Rouge, New Orleans, Biloxi, and Mobile, and was the only official parish road until 1843. **Bogue Chitto River** near Franklinton is popular for tubing, canoeing, and fishing. Public access.

I-55 SOUTHBOUND, LOUISIANA TOURIST INFORMATION CENTER: near Kentwood, offers information, maps, and brochures, as well as picnic and rest area. Open daily except holidays, 8:30-5. (504-229-8338)

CAMP MOORE STATE COMMEMORATIVE AREA: U.S. 51, in the community of Tangipahoa. This small, 4-acre site was one of the largest Confederate training grounds in the South. The Confederate Museum with artifacts from the Civil War and Confederate cemetery are not currently open. Inquire.

AMITE: U.S. 51, is a small town with a vintage southern-style Victorian architectural district. **The Episcopal Church of the Incarnation,** 111 Olive, built in 1908 to replace an 1872 edifice destroyed by a tornado,is an excellent example of small-town Gothic ecclesiastical architecture. **Blythewood Plantation,** 300 Elm, on a Spanish land grant, is a dogtrot-style Victorian home, completed in 1895. It replaced a Greek Revival house built in the early 19th centurythat burned. Located on a lovely 10-acre tract with spring-fed lake and furnished with antiques. By appt. Admission. (504-748-8621). **Amite Oyster Festival,** held the third weekend in March, offers arts and crafts, music and dancing, oyster eating, tug of war, greased pig contest. **Tangipahoa River** is a popular recreational area for canoeing, camping, picnicking. Beaches. Equipment rentals and shuttle service available.

INDEPENDENCE: U.S. 51 at La. 40, was established in the 1880s as a result of the building of the railroad. Numerous Italians settled in the area, attracted by the strawberry industry. **The historic district** contains an interesting collection of early-20th-century residential and commercial architecture. **Italian Cultural Museum,** housed in a turn-of-the-century church, features exhibits of area Italian history, culture, and heritage. By appt. (504-878-4664). **Italian Festival,** last weekend in April, features cultural exhibits and entertainment, including food and street dancing. **The Natalbany River** flows south into Lake Maurepas and is popular for fishing and water sports.

LORANGER: La. 40 and 1062, hosts Old Farmer's Day, held the third weekend in October, featuring exhibits of farm life a century ago, including field work with draft horses, horse and mule pulling contests, wood stove cooking, moonshine still, syrup making, fence-rail splitting, etc. (504-878-9343)

FOLSOM AREA: Zemurray Gardens, on La. 40, is a 75-acre garden in a pine forest that includes natural landscaping, as well as azaleas, camellias, and dogwoods, a 20-acre lake, and nature trails. Open late March to mid-April. 10-6. Admission. (504-878-6731). **Global Wildlife Center,** La. 40 east of Zemurray, features covered-wagon tours to view endangered and threatened wildlife, especially hoof stock, in an open environment. 10-5, daily. Admission. (504) 624-WILD.

HAMMOND: on U.S. 51 and 190, founded when the railroad was laid in 1854, became a shoemaking center for the Confederacy during the Civil War and was for many years called the Strawberry Capital. **The Tangipahoa Tourist Commission,** 2612 S. Morrison, offers information, tours, maps, and brochures. Open weekdays, 8-4. (504-542-7520). **The Hammond Cultural Foundation**, downtown Hammond, offers information on special exhibits, performances, and events and features changing art exhibits. Tues.-Fri., 12-4; weekends, 10-4. (504-542-7113). **The Hammond National Register Historic District** preserves a collection of turn-of-the-century buildings, mainly brick with early-20th-century façades. **The Illinois Central Gulf Railroad Depot,** built in 1912, first used to ship strawberries, is a fine example of small-town railroad architecture. It still functions as a passenger depot for Amtrak. **Grace Memorial Episcopal Church,** founded in 1866 and consecrated in 1888, is a fine example of rural Gothic architecture. **Southeastern Louisiana University,** founded in 1925, includes Clark Hall Gallery, featuring changing art exhibits. For more campus information, (504-549-2000). **Louisiana Balloon Festival and Airshow,** held in May, features hot air balloon races, airshow and special plane and aviation displays, carnival, entertainment, and food.

PONCHATOULA: U.S. 51 at La. 22. The name is derived from the Choctaw Indian word for "hanging hair," for the abundance of Spanish moss on the trees. The town was incorporated in 1861. It now bills itself as "America's Antique City" with a concentration of antique shops in the downtown area. **Ponchatoula Country Market,** housed in the train depot, built in 1895, features crafts, homemade jellies, and collectibles in the old railroad station. The restored baggage-mail car features an exhibit of local artists, as well as a restored **Railway Post Office Museum.** A restored 1912 steam locomotive, once used to haul cypress logs from the nearby swamp, completes the complex. Open Mon.-Sat., 10-5; Sun, 12-5. (504-386-9580). **Collinswood School Museum,** across the street from the depot, is a century-old, one-room schoolhouse with historical artifacts and memorabilia. Open same hours as Country Market. **Kliebert's Alligator Farm tours,** W. Yellow

Water Road, north of Ponchatoula, open Mar. 1-Nov. 1 daily, noon to dark. Admission. (504-345-3617). **Ponchatoula Strawberry Festival,** held thesecond weekend in April, celebrates the unique Louisiana strawberry with eating contests, auction, banks, parade, carnival. **Scenic drive:** La. 22 west from Ponchatoula to Springfield passes antebellum and turn-of-the-century homes and picturesque property with large oak trees.

MADISONVILLE: La. 22, in St. Tammany Parish, was founded in 1811 and is the southern gateway to the Natchez Trace. Named for Chief Tammanend, a Delaware Indian declared by English admirers as their patron saint, the parish is on the Tchefuncte (pronounced "chuh-funk-ta") River. The picturesque turn-of-the-century town under moss-draped oaks offers public access to the recreational facilities of the river. Fishing, water skiing, boating. **Madisonville Museum.** 21 Cedar Street, is housed in the old courthouse, built in 1911, and features Civil War, wildlife, and Indian culture exhibits. Open Sat., 10-4; Sun., 12-4; and by appt. (504-845-2100). **Bayou Cottage,** built in 1807, is the oldest home extant in the area. Private; drive-by. **Fairview-Riverside State Park,** La. 22, is a 98-acre park on the Tchefuncte River 2 miles east of Madisonville, offering fishing, skiing, camping, boating, picnicking. (504-845-3318). **Otis House**, located within the park, was built in the 1930s. Open Fri.-Sun., 11-4. Admission. (504-845-8043). **Wooden Boat Festival** held annually in September.

COVINGTON: U.S. 190, originally settled by Englishmen in the mid-18th century, is one of the resort centers of the ozone belt, reputed to be especially healthful because of the pine trees. St. Tammany Parish tourist information available at 600 N. U.S. 90. (504-892-0520). **St. Joseph's Abbey,** off La. 25, is a Benedictine monastery containing frescoes in the chapel and refectory by Fr. Dom Gregory deWit. Open 8-11 and 1:30-5. **Christ Episcopal Church,** established in 1846 and dedicated by Bishop Leonidas Polk, built in Queen Anne ecclesiastical style. Has a large, octagonal bell tower and features handhewn pews, a small slave gallery, and 8 of the 10 flags flown over the parish. **Lee Lane historic district** is an area of small, restored turn-of-the-century shotgun houses and cottages. **Smith's Hardware Museum**, 308 N. Columbia, features local artifacts and exhibits. Open weekdays, 8:30-5. **St. Tammany Art Association**, 129 N. New Hampshire, features changing exhibits of local and regional artists. Tues.-Sat., 10-4; Sun., 1-4. (504-892-8650). **Bogue Falaya rivers** (Big and Little) offer parks and recreational sites for swimming, fishing, boating. **St. Tammany Parish Fair,** held the first weekend in November, is a country fair featuring rodeo events, carnival, food, and entertainment. Admission. (504-892-2208). The drive from Covington to Folsom on La. 25 is scenic, passing through the heart of Louisiana's thoroughbred horse farms and a center of the horticultural industry.

LAKE PONTCHARTRAIN CAUSEWAY: the 24-mile span crosses Lake Pontchartrain, a large (635 square miles), brackish body named by Iberville in honor of his French minister of finance. This is the longest continuous overwater bridge in the world. The causeway connects St. Tammany Parish on the north shore with Jefferson Parish, just beyond the Orleans line. Toll.

MANDEVILLE: U.S. 190 on Lake Pontchartrain, was developed in the 1840s as a popular summer resort. Many of the lovely homes are still in use. **Seven Sisters Oak,** the largest and oldest live oak in the state, a member of the Live Oak Society, is on private property near Lake Pontchartrain. Only the back of the tree can be seen from the road. **Seafood Festival,** held spring or summer, features a carnival, games, music, and a food tent with seafood booths. **Fontainebleau State Park,** U.S. 190 east, is on the site of an old sugar mill built in 1829. The ruins still remain. Day-use area of the park is on Lake Pontchartrain, offering a beach, swimming, boating, picnicking, explicated nature trail through diverse habitats. Group camping and primitive camping. Admission. (504-624-4443)

ABITA SPRINGS: La. 36, is the center of the "ozone belt," the site of medicinal water springs. **The Abita Springs Pavilion,** Main, built in 1888, is an octagonal Victorian bandstand in a park, on the site of the springs.

LACOMBE: U.S. 190, grew up along Bayou Lacombe near an early Catholic mission established to work with the Choctaw Indians. **Our Lady of Lourdes Shrine,** Fish Hatchery Road, was built in the early 1900s by Fr. Francois Balay as a replica of the Shrine at Lourdes, France, commemorating a vision by St. Bernadette. The shrine is located in a wooded glen. Open daylight hours. **Bayou Lacombe Museum,** 1 block off U.S. 190, housed in a 2-room schoolhouse built in 1912, features exhibits of vintage furniture, jewelry, kitchen equipment and furnishings, Choctaw Indian artifacts, and other memorabilia of the area. Open every Sun., 2-5, from March through Oct.; first Sun. of the month, Nov.-Feb. Donation. (504-882-5364 or 7218). **Scenic district:** along Main Street and Fish Hatchery Road, where numerous vintage homes and old oak trees remain. **Bayou Lacombe Crab Festival,** held the last weekend in June at the park, features live entertainment, contests, crab races, arts and crafts, Bayou Lacombe Rural Museum exhibits, and food booths.

SLIDELL: U.S. 11, founded in 1888, includes a renovated, turn-of-the-century district reflecting the town's heritage, including old town jail, built in the 1860s. The commission offers information, maps, brochures, and tours. Open weekdays, 8:30-5. (504-649-0730). **The Slidell Cultural Arts Center**, Erlanger at Third Street, features changing local and travelling art exhibits. (504-646-4375). **Cultural Commission** offers information on special performances, exhibits, and events in the area. (504-646-4375). **St. Joe Brick Works**, U.S. 11 north, offers tours by appt. of the craft of brickmaking. (504-863-6161)

PEARL RIVER AREA: the Pearl River forms the eastern boundary line of the state in this area. **The Bogue Chitto National Wildlife Refuge,** off La. 41 near Sun, is an 18,000-acre tract of unique bottomland hardwood. Fishing, canoeing, camping. Hunting in season. Guided canoe trips and canoe rentals available, off La. 41, Isabel Swamp Road (504-735-1173) **I-10 westbound Louisiana Tourist Information Center** offers information, maps , and brochures, picnic and rest areas. Open daily except holidays, 8:30-5. (504-863-7260). The town of Pearl River hosts the **Pearl River Catfish Festival,** held in late spring, featuring games, music, carnival, and fried catfish. **Pearl River Wildlife Management Area,** a 26,000-acre tract of swampland, is accessible largely by boat. Hunting, fishing, trapping by permit, bird-watching, and camping. **The Honey Island Swamp Nature Trail,** located on the east bank of the river in the wildlife management area, is a self-guided, 1-mile, walking trail. Insect repellent advised. (504-342-5875). **Honey Island Swamp tours** by boat available. Inquire at St. Tammany Tourist Commission. **The White Kitchen wetlands area,** a holding of the Louisiana Nature Conservancy, is located off U.S. 90 and 190. Accessible by water only, the pristine wilderness habitat of swamp, marsh, and slash-pine/hardwood supports an extraordinary diversity of flora and fauna. Access arranged. (504-338-1040 or 504-641-1769)

FORT PIKE STATE COMMEMORATIVE AREA: U.S. 90 (Old Spanish Trail). A masonry fortress on a 125-acre site, built from 1818 to 1827 as part of President James Madison's plan of national defense. The fort overlooks the Rigolets (pronounced "rig-o-leez"), a natural channel between Lake Pontchartrain and Lake Borgne, an arm of the Gulf of Mexico, and is designed to withstand attack from land or sea. It retains the pure design of enclosed casemates (vaults within the walls) along exit tunnels. Both Confederate and Union troops occupied the fort during the Civil War. A museum and interpretive program, picnic areas, and boat launch. Admission. (504-662-5703)

FORT MACOMB: paired with Fort Pike, this masonry fort protected the Chef Menteur Pass, another entrance to Lake Pontchartrain from the gulf. It was built in 1820-28. Gen. Andrew Jackson had placed a battery here in 1815. Today it is in ruins, partially submerged by the waters of the Chef, and is off-limits to the public due to hazardous conditions.

NEW ORLEANS: New Orleans' international reputation as the Big Easy—epicenter of food, jazz, Mardi Gras, and fun—sometimes overwhelms its equally rich heritage of history and culture. But it is the two facets of the city together that create the unique flavor that charms both visitors and residents. The city is squeezed into an area between the south shore of Lake Pontchartrain and the curves of the Mississippi River on the south, or to the west, depending on your location—which is why natives often explain directions in terms of uptown, downtown, lakeside, and riverside, instead of north, south, east, and west. The city is comprised of many originally separate, interesting historic districts and enclaves, some of which can be seen by walking; other parts are best appreciated by driving. Tours and/or brochures for self-guided tours are available. **The Greater New Orleans Tourist and Convention Commission,** in the Superdome, offers information, maps, brochures, guides, and tours. Open daily, 8:30-5. (504-566-5011). **The Louisiana Office of Tourism,** 529 St. Ann, offers information, maps, brochures, and guides. **The Arts Council of New Orleans** offers information on special exhibits, performances, and events in the area. (504-523-1465). **The Preservation Resource Center,** 604 Julia Street, offers information and tours on historic architecture, neighborhoods, and preservation. (504-581-7032)

THE FRENCH QUARTER AND ENVIRONS: the Vieux Carré, or old square, was laid out in 1721 in a symmetrical shape as a fortified city by Adrian de Pauger. It is bounded today by the river and three streets, Canal, Rampart, and Esplanade, creating a very European village effect. The architecture in the French Quarter is a unique mixture of French and Spanish styles, including the characteristic wrought-or cast-iron decoration, as well as American influences. In the late 1930s, after a period of deterioration, the Vieux Carré Commission was established to protect the integrity of the remaining buildings and regulate new construction. **Jackson Square,** the old Place d'Armes (a military parade ground), was established in 1721. The statue of Andrew Jackson was erected in 1856 and the square renamed. Artists, street performers, and musicians surround the square, where the streets have become pedestrian malls. **St. Louis Basilica,** formerly St. Louis Cathedral, built in 1794 to replace an earlier church that burned, was constructed in the Spanish style but subsequently

Andrew Jackson statue in Jackson Square, New Orleans. (Courtesy Louisiana Office of Tourism)

was remodeled in 1851 to its present appearance. It is actually a basilica and the oldest active cathedral in the country, features many original furnishings and frescoes. Open daily, guided tours, 9-5; Sun., 1:30-5 after mass.

The Louisiana State Museum is one of the finest historical museums in the country and consists of the following facilities (all charge admission): *The Cabildo,* 751 Chartres Street, on the uptown side of the cathedral, was built in 1795 as the seat of Spanish rule. The Louisiana Purchase transaction took place here. The permanent collection includes significant artifacts from Louisiana, New Orleans, and Mississippi River exploration, history, and settlement. Because of a fire, which caused extensive damage to the roof and uppermost story in May 1988, the Cabildo is closed to the public. Restoration is underway. *The Presbytere* (Priest's House), begun in 1794 and completed in 1813, was never used as the priest's residence but housed the Lousiana Supreme Court in the early 19th century and now exhibits collections of costumes, textiles, decorative arts, and historic photos, as well as special displays. Open Wed.-Sun., 10-5. *The Old U.S. Mint,* 400 Esplanade, built in 1836, is the nation's oldest, unreconstructed mint on its original site and includes permanent exhibits on Mardi Gras and New Orleans jazz and houses an extensive research library and archives. Open Wed.-Sun., 10-5. *1850 House,* 523 St. Ann, a restored 19th-century townhouse in the Lower Pontalba Building, which, with the Upper Pontalba, are the oldest apartment complex in the country, constructed in 1848-50 in Renaissance Revival style with ornate decorative grillwork along wide galleries. The museum house has been restored and furnished to the period.

Jackson House, built in 1842, *the Arsenal,* built in 1839, and *Creole House,* built in 1842, 619 St. Peter, are holdings of the museum. *Madame John's Legacy,* 632 Dumaine, built in 1788, is the finest surviving example of a French colonial raised townhouse. Renovated and furnished with an outstanding collection of colonial Louisiana furnishings and exhibits of social history. Open Wed.-Sun., 10-6. Walking tours of the French Quarter by the Friends of the Cabildo are offered Tues.-Sun., 9:30 & 1:30; Mon. at 1:30. Admission. Tours start in 1850 House. (504-523-3939). **Jackson Brewery,** a century-old building that housed a beer brewery, has been converted into a festival marketplace. **The Moon Walk** is a section of the Mississippi River levee across from Jackson Square that serves as a promenade overlooking the river. Nearby is one of the docks for tour boat cruises that explore the river and nearby bayous. (504-586-8777 or 586-0740). Downriver is **Woldenberg Riverfront Park,** a landscaped river overlook. **Aquarium of**

the Americas, 1 Canal Street at the river, one of the world's major aquarium facilities, features over 10,000 species of fish and other aquafauna, birds, and reptiles in exhibits such as the Gulf of Mexico, Mississippi River Delta, Caribbean Reef, and others. Open daily. Admission. (504-861-2537). A riverfront streetcar line runs along the river from Esplanade Avenue to the Riverwalk. **French Market,** 800-1000 Decatur, originally the marketplace site of the Choctaw Indians, is a series of colonnaded buildings constructed in stages from 1813 to 1872 that served as markets for produce,dairy, butchers, etc. Now renovated and glamorized, the buildings house shops, a Farmers' Market, the original Cafe du Monde coffee and beignet cafe, a weekend flea market, and the **Jean Lafitte National Historical Park headquarters.** Headquartered at 916 N. Peters, Louisiana's only national park is composed of several units. The French Quarter Unit is a cultural interpretive center, which sponsors guided walking tours daily, focusing on the history of New Orleans and the French Quarter, the Garden District, and specialized subject tours. Heritage cooking demonstrations and musical performances are presented on weekends. (504-589-2636)

Ursuline Convent, 1114 Chartres, completed in 1794, is the oldest building in the city. The convent housed the Ursuline nuns, who conducted the first Catholic school in Louisiana, the first Indian and Negro school, and the first Catholic orphanage. The building has been the archbishopric for the diocese. It now houses archives of the church. On the grounds is St. Mary's Italian Church, erected circa 1846. **Beauregard-Keyes House,** 1113 Chartres, is a Greek Revival house dating from 1826, formerly occupied by Confederate Gen. P. G. T. Beauregard and author Frances Parkinson Keyes. Open Mon.-Sat., 10-3. Admission. (504-523-7257)

Gallier House, 1132 Royal, built circa 1857 by renowned architect James Gallier, is restored and furnished as a mid-19th-century urban townhouse. Interpretive programs and special events. Open Mon.-Sat., 10-4:30. Admission. (504-523-6722). **Hermann-Grima House,** 820 St. Louis, built in 1831, is one of the earliest and best examples of American architecture in the French Quarter. The complex includes the 3-story mansion in eastern seaboard style, garçonniere, open-hearth kitchen, stable, and 2 courtyards. Living history. Open Mon.-Sat., 10-4. Admission. (504-525-5661). **Historic New Orleans Collection,** 533 Royal, is a complex of buildings including an exhibition gallery, 2 museum residences, and research center with historic maps, prints, drawings, and documents. Tours of the Merieult House, built in 1792. Tues.-Sat., 10-4:30. Admission. (504-523-4662). **Old**

Pharmacy Museum, 514 Chartres, built in 1823 as a pharmacy, now exhibits an extensive collection of vintage apothecary items, medical instruments and equipment, bottles, voodoo potions, and patio herb garden. Open Tues.-Sun., 10-5. Admission. (524-9077). **New Orleans Spring Fiesta House,** 826 St. Ann, is a restored and furnished 19th-century townhouse. Open Mon.-Fri., 1-4. Admission. Headquarters for the New Orleans Spring Fiesta, held second weekend in April, featuring a tour of historic homes and courtyards. Admission. (504-581-1367). **Historic Voodoo Museum,** 724 Dumaine, presents exhibits on the history of voodoo in New Orleans. Open Sun.-Thurs., 10-dusk; Fri. and Sat., 10-10. Admission. (504-523-7685)

Musee Conti Historical Wax Museum, 917 Conti, is a collection of wax tableaus and figures representing historic events and people. Open daily, 10-5:30. Admission. **Germaine Wells Mardi Gras Museum,** 813 Bienville, exhibits a collection of Carnival court gowns and costumes. Open daily. **Preservation Hall,** 726 St. Peter, is the prototype old-fashioned jazz hall. Admission during performances.

Lafitte's Blacksmith Shop, 941 Bourbon, built circa 1780 with briquette-entre-poteaux construction, was reportedly the business front for pirate Jean Lafitte's smuggling operation. **The Church of Our Lady of Guadalupe,** 411 N. Rampart, was built as a mortuary chapel in 1826 after a yellow fever epidemic. All funerals of French Quarter residents were performed there from 1827 to 1860. The International Shrine of St. Jude adjoins the building, containing statues, artifacts, and mosaics. **Bourbon Street** and **Royal Street** are two famed thoroughfares, the former for nightlife, the latter for antiques shops and galleries. Historic buildings and sites in the French Quarter are too extensive to list further individually. Request specialized block-by-block maps and texts that explicate architecture, historic events, literary connections, courtyards, etc., available for self-guided touring or guided tours. **French Quarter Festival,** held the 2nd weekend in April, features patio tours, fireworks, steamboat race, children's activities, music, food. (504-522-5730). **Tennessee Williams/New Orleans Literary Festival,** held the last weekend in March, offers theatre, literary walking tours, book fair, panel discussions. **St. Joseph Day Parade** is the culmination of the celebration of St. Joseph Day, held 3rd Saturday in March. Catholics of Sicilian descent build altars of food, decorated with greenery, flowers, and candles in thanks to St. Joseph. Many are in churches, though some families build them at home.

Faubourg Marigny, developed in 1806, was the first Creole suburb in New Orleans, and is still considered an area of considerable architectural integrity. The Nathan-Lewis-Cizek House, a Greek Revival

French Quarter courtyard at 520 Royal Street. (Courtesy Louisiana Office of Tourism)

cottage, and Rising Sun House, a Victorian Creole cottage, 2020 Burgundy, are examples of the architectural styles in this historic district laid out in an angled grid pattern from Esplanade to Press Street. Washington Park is a picturesque, landscaped square.

Louisiana Military History Museum and State Weapons Collection, housed at Jackson Barracks, 6437 St. Claude, in Orleans Parish at the St. Bernard Parish line. It exhibits military history, weapons, and uniforms from all 9 wars in which Louisiana has fought, in a powder magazine built in 1837. Open weekdays, 8-4 by appt. for large groups. (504-278-6242)

DOWNTOWN AND THE CENTRAL BUSINESS DISTRICT: Downtown means Canal Street—171 feet from curb to curb, one of the widest streets in the world. **The Canal Street ferry** crosses the Mississippi River from the foot of Canal Street, depositing passengers at Algiers Point, an interesting neighborhood of 19th-century churches, shotguns, and 2-storied, galleried houses. Certain boat tours also depart from here, including one to the zoo. (504-586-8777). From the ferry is a good view of a small part of the Port of New Orleans, one of the largest international cargo ports in the country. **U.S. Customs House,** 423 Canal, begun in 1848 but not completed until 1913(!), was used as Union headquarters during the occupation of New Orleans in the Civil War. An impressive example of neoclassic public architecture. **The World Trade Center** at the foot of Canal Street houses consulates and trade commissions, with a rotunda of international flags in the lobby and an observation deck on the 31st floor. (Admission to deck). **Piazza d'Italia,** Poydras at Tchoupitoulas, completed in 1978, features representations of the five orders of Italian architecture and the St. Joseph's Fountain. The American Italian Museum and Research Library, 537 S. Peters behind the Piazza, features exhibitions of Italian-American subjects. Open Wed.-Fri., 10-4; Sat., 10-1. Donation. (504-522-7294 or 891-1904). At the foot of Poydras, the site of the 1984 World's Fair is now partially occupied by **Riverwalk festival marketplace** and the **Ernest N. Morial Convention Center.** A tour boat dock for cruises of the river and bayous is located here. (504-524-1814)

St. Charles Avenue Streetcar stop, corner of Carondelet and Canal, is the official termination point of the St. Charles streetcar loop before it continues its circuit. **Saenger Theatre,** 1111 Canal, built in 1927, now a performance theatre, is decorated in fantasy-baroque style with marble, statuary, painted sky-ceiling, and organ. Open during performances. **The Orpheum Theatre,** 125 University Pl., built in 1918 in the Beaux Arts style, now a performing arts hall, features elaborate terra-cotta decoration and interior dome. Open during

Downtown New Orleans and the Mississippi River. (Courtesy Louisiana Office of Tourism)

performances. **Gallier Hall,** 545 St. Charles, begun in 1845 and dedicated in 1853, served as New Orleans City Hall for 100 years. Now a city office building and considered one of the most beautiful Greek Revival public buildings in the country, it was named for its architect, James Gallier.

Lafayette Square, 500 block of Camp, was the city center of the "new American" development after 1803 when the newcomers developed their own community outside the French Quarter. **Julia Row,** Julia Street, is an intact row of Federal-Greek Revival townhouses built in the 1830s, designed by James Dakin, with commercial space on the ground floor and residences on the upper floor. **Louisiana Children's Museum,** 428 Julia, offers a series of exciting hands-on exhibits and play areas for children to learn through exploration; also special visiting exhibits. Open Tues.-Sun., 9:30-4:30. Closed holidays. Admission. (504-523-1357). **St. Patrick's Church,** 724 Camp, built in 1840 in Gothic Revival style, is the second oldest church in New Orleans and was designed by Charles and James Dakin. **Contemporary Arts Center,** 900 Camp, features exhibits of contemporary arts, crafts, other visual media, and performing arts. Open Wed.-Sun., 11-5. Admission. (504-523-1216)

Lee Circle, 1000 St. Charles, is the meeting place of four thoroughfares, centered by an 1884 statue of Gen. Robert E. Lee, facing north. **K&B Plaza,** 1055 St. Charles, features an outdoor and lobby display of contemporary sculpture. **Confederate Museum,** 929 Camp, displays Civil War uniforms, flags, weapons, portraits, medical equipment, and other memorabilia. Open Mon.-Sat., 10-4. Admission. (504-523-4522). **Louisiana Superdome,** opened in 1975, is a 52-acre-under-roof multipurpose facility equipped to handle sports events, trade shows, and activities. The domed stadium is home of Louisiana's only professional football team, the New Orleans Saints, and site of the annual NCAA post-season Sugar Bowl Classic. Tours of the Superdome are available daily, 10, 12, 2, and 4, except during some events. Admission for tours. (504-587-3808). **Mardi Gras** in New Orleans is a lengthy celebration of balls and parades. Many of the parades take place down St. Charles Avenue through the Central Business District and begin two weekends before Fat Tuesday. Mardi Gras day is called the Greatest Free Show on Earth, an all-day celebration with parades, costumes, and partying in the streets. **La Fête** is a week-long celebration in early July, featuring a culinary exhibit and food booths, concerts, film festival, performing and visual arts, boat races on the river, and more. (504-525-4143)

GARDEN DISTRICT AREA: Coliseum Square, running from

Melpomene to Race, was laid out in the 1830s as a park. The Coliseum Square district, the city's oldest garden neighborhood, features antebellum houses and churches, including St. Mary's Assumption Church, Josephine at Erato, built in 1858. **Grace King House,** 1749 Coliseum, built in 1849, a Greek Revival home remodeled in 1871, where the author lived from 1904 to 1932. Drive-by. **The Garden District** is an area formally bounded by Jackson, Louisiana, St. Charles, and Magazine streets. Originally the city of Lafayette, which was laid out in the late 1830s, this is where the American elite had their homes. Greek Revival and mid-Victorian residential architecture are featured, including classical columns and wrought-iron or cast-iron ornamentation. *Women's Opera Guild House,* 2504 Prytania, is a pre-Civil War Greek Revival and Italianate mansion furnished in early-19th-century and Victorian pieces. Open by appt. Admission. (Closed in the summer). (504-899-1945). *Holiday Home Tour,* sponsored by the Preservation Resource Center, offers one of the rare opportunities to see interiors of select Garden District and St. Charles Avenue mansions. Admission. (504-581-7032). *Trinity Church,* 1329 Jackson, built in 1851 in English Gothic style with Victorian adaptation, numbers Bishop Leonidas Polk among its early leaders. *Lafayette Cemetery #1,* Washington at Prytania, was established in 1833 and features fine cast-iron gates and above-ground tombs, including those of many Civil War veterans.

Many Garden District homes have historic or architectural interest. Several highlights follow; for more detailed maps and guides, ask the tourism centers or Preservation Resource Center. *1313 8th,* raised plantation cottage, home of George Washington Cable, where Mark Twain often visited. *2343 Prytania,* built in 1870, now a girls' school. *1134 First,* built in 1849-50, where Jefferson Davis died. *2340 Prytania,* thought to be the oldest house still standing in the area, built in 1838. *1448 Fourth,* built in 1859 in modified Italian villa style, with a cornstalk ornamental ironwork fence. **Irish Channel,** a neighborhood between Constance and the river, extending from St. Joseph to Louisiana Avenue, established in the early 19th century, one of the rough sections of town, was settled by a large Irish population in 1840, followed by a number of Germans. Some of the finer homes in this area were located around Annunciation Square. The St. Patrick's Day Parade and Celebration takes place here on March 17. **Magazine Street** runs from Canal Street where the Spanish powder magazine stood, through the warehouse area of the Central Business District, the Irish Channel and Garden District, to the Audubon Zoo. A ride along Magazine Street offers a telescoped view of New Orleans history and its architecture and development. There are many antique and specialty shops along Magazine.

UPTOWN: Audubon Park, 6400-6900 St. Charles, a 400-acre urban park named for naturalist John James Audubon, was established on the site of a sugar plantation owned by Etienne de Boré and was the location of the Great Cotton Exposition in 1884. The park offers walking and jogging paths, lagoons, scenic drive, picnicking, golf course, and tennis courts. *Audubon Zoological Gardens,* 6500 Magazine, located on 58 acres between Magazine and the river, features over 1,000 animals in natural settings, sea-lion feedings, elephant rides, Children's Village, reptile encounter, Louisiana swamp exhibit, and other developed areas. Open Mon.-Fri., 9:30-4:30; weekends, 9:30-5:30. Admission (504-861-2537). Behind the zoo is a viewing pavilion and dock on the Mississippi River levee where a tour boat from the downtown area lands.

Tulane University, 6823 St. Charles, was established in 1884. Housed in the university's *Howard-Tilton Memorial Library* is the Amistad Research Center containing archives, documents, papers, and artwork pertaining to the history of blacks in America. The library also houses extensive Latin American and jazz history archives. Open Mon.-Fri., 8:30-5:00; Sat., 1-5. (504-865-5535). *Middle American Research Institute,* 4th floor of Dinwiddie Hall, exhibits artifacts of Mayan, Aztec, Toltec, and other Central American cultures. Open weekdays, 8:30-4. (865-5110). *Newcomb College Art Department Gallery* features exhibits, including the art-nouveau-style Newcomb pottery. For campus information about special exhibits, performances, sports, or events, call (504-865-5714).

Loyola University, 6363 St. Charles, next door to Tulane, was established here in 1904, the largest Catholic university in the South. For campus information about special exhibits, performances, sports, or events, call (504-865-2011 or 865-3529). **Old Carrollton Courthouse,** 719 S. Carrollton, built in 1855 as the administrative center of the town of Carrollton, which was incorporated into New Orleans in 1874. Recently used as a public high school. **Ursuline Convent and Academy,** 2635 State, founded in 1727, is one of the oldest schools for girls in the country. The museum contains letters of Thomas Jefferson and James Madison, a memento carved by Padre Cirillo for Oliver Pollock in 1779, and other artifacts. Site of the national shrine of Our Lady of Prompt Succor. By appt. Admission. (504-866-1472). **Xavier University,** Palmetto Street, was established in 1915 to offer Catholic-oriented education to black youth. For campus information on special exhibits, performances, and events, call (504-483-7357).

BAYOU ST. JOHN AND LAKEFRONT AREA: Esplanade Ridge Historic District, from behind the French Quarter extending to Bayou St. John, first developed in the 1830s, was the French equivalent of the American Garden District. It still includes a number of elegant homes and cottages that can be viewed by taking the public bus. Edgar Degas, the only Impressionist painter ever to reside in the United States, lived at 2306 Esplanade.

Fair Grounds Race Track, Gentilly Boulevard, founded in 1872, the 3rd oldest racetrack in the country, features thoroughbred racing and pari-mutuel betting. Open Wed.-Sun., Thanksgiving to April. No minors. Admission. (504-944-5515)

The Fair Grounds is the site of the **New Orleans Jazz and Heritage Festival,** held for 2 weekends plus weeknights in late April, including nationally known musicians performing jazz, rhythm and blues, Cajun, country, folk, ragtime, and other genres, as well as concerts in other locations. Louisiana cuisine booths and native arts and crafts exhibits. Admission. (504-522-4786). **Dillard University,** Gentilly Boulevard, founded in 1935, is a primarily black institution of higher learning on a beautiful 63-acre campus. For campus information on special exhibits, performances, and events, call (504-286-4734). **Louisiana Nature and Science Center,** 11000 Lake Forest Boulevard in New Orleans East, features hands-on nature and science exhibits, wilderness area, walking trail, guided walks, interpretive programs, and planetarium. Planetarium shows daily. Center open Tues.-Fri., 9-5; weekends, noon-5. Admission. (504-246-5672). **Lakefront,** along the shore of Lake Pontchartrain, is a park featuring picnicking and seawall. Mardi Gras Fountain, a changing water show in a fountain decorated with Mardi Gras krewe plaques, is especially effective after dark. **University of New Orleans (UNO)** was founded in 1958. The 10,000-seat Lakefront Arena hosts concerts, theatre productions, and sporting events. For campus information on special exhibits, performances, or events, call (504-286-6000 or 286-6805). **Southern Yacht Club,** West End, was founded in 1849, the 2nd oldest in the country. Private. **Bucktown,** west Lakeshore along the 17th Street Canal, is a late-19th-century fishing village, now part of Metairie, that features a combination of quaint buildings.

Spanish Fort, Beauregard Street, is a brick fortification built in 1770 for the Spanish defense of the area. The area became a resort in 1823. The foundations of the fort remain. **City Park,** a 1,500-acre urban park, offers picnicking and recreational facilities, tennis courts, four 18-hole golf courses and double-decker driving range, horse stables for individual or group lessons, boat rentals, and fishing permits for lagoons. *Dueling Oaks,* near the New Orleans Museum of Art, was the scene of many duels to settle arguments and matters of honor in the late 1700s and much of the 1800s. *Amusement area* includes: a renovated, hand-carved wooden carousel, built in 1906, the only one in the state; a 1.3-mile minitrain ride; roller coaster, bumper cars, and ferris wheel; Storyland, a Children's Fairy Tale Theme Park with educational programs and entertainment. Open daily, 10-3 (summer hours may be longer). New Orleans Botanical Garden, 7 acres of formal landscape with fountains and sculpture. Admission. *Celebration in the Oaks,* a festival of Christmas lights, is held in the Botanical Garden from the first weekend in December through Christmas, 5-10:30 P.M. (504-482-4888)

New Orleans Museum of Art, in City Park, built in 1911, features a permanent collection including works of western civilization from the pre-Christian era to the present, featuring Impressionism, Louisiana genre, 20th-century European and American painting and sculpture, portrait miniatures, early American furniture, Italian painting, Chinese jade, glass, and African, Asian, and pre-Columbian art. Special exhibits on a continuing basis. Docent tours and educational programs. Open Tues.-Sun. except holidays, 10-5. Admission. (504-488-2631). **Bayou St. John** connected the lake with an old Indian path to the river. In the early 1800s, a canal was dug to extend the bayou to a basin near what is now the Municipal Auditorium. Some of Louisiana's earliest settlers' plantations were located in this area. **Pitot House,** 1440 Moss, is a restored late-18th-century West Indian-style plantation home furnished to the period for aristocratic owners. James Pitot, second mayor of New Orleans, lived here. Open Wed.-Sat., 10-3. Admission. (504-482-0312). **Longue Vue House and Gardens,** 7 Bamboo Road, is a 20th-century private estate on 7 acres furnished with English and American antiques with a gallery of modern and contemporary art. The formal gardens are in bloom all year, with fountains and sculpture. Open Tues.-Sat., 10-4:30; Sun., 1-5. Admission. (504-488-5488)

JEFFERSON PARISH, EAST BANK: an extension of the New Orleans Metro Area, consisting of contiguous communities that create one of the Crescent City's most interesting suburbs. Created as a parish in 1825, it is on both sides of the Mississippi River, extending from Lake Pontchartrain to the Gulf of Mexico at Grand Isle. **Jefferson Parish Tourist Information Center,** I-10 and Loyola Drive, Kenner, is open from 8 A.M. to 5:30 P.M. 7 days a week. (504-468-8227). **Camp Parapet Powder Magazine,** Arlington Street off U.S. 90, built in 1862 as part of the Confederate fortifications but captured by the Union

Army, is now restored to its Civil War configuration. By appt. (504-468-8227). **Huey P. Long Bridge,** joining East and West Jefferson, crosses the Mississippi River between Jefferson and Bridge City. **Elmwood Plantation,** River Road, built in the mid-1700s in French Colonial style with gun slots in the first floor, is surrounded by 22 oaks over 200 years old. The house is in ruins as the result of a 1978 fire; a 19th-century barn stands on the property. **Lafreniere Park,** Downs Boulevard in Metairie, is a 155-acre tract that offers recreational facilities, lagoons, a pavilion for outdoor performances, and a nature area for bird-watching, picnicking. **Linear Park,** along Lake Pontchartrain, is a 10-mile recreation strip between the lake and the levee for jogging, bicycling, walking, fishing. Vehicular access and boat launching at Williams Boulevard, Kenner, and Bonnabel Boulevard, Metairie. Parking access limited.

Rivertown, adjacent to the river in Kenner, is a complex of renovated cottages and commercial buildings, some from the turn of the century. A collection of city-owned museums are open Tues.-Sat., 9-5; Sun., 1-5. Admission. (504-468-7274). *The Louisiana Wildlife and Fisheries Museum,* 303 Williams, exhibits over 700 preserved specimens of Louisiana wildlife, including several natural habitat displays. Also, a 15,000-gallon saltwater aquarium with a variety of marine life from Louisiana waters. *The Louisiana Toy Train Museum,* 519 Williams, in a store built in 1916, displays railroad documents, photos and artifacts, model train layouts, and a hands-on streetcar exhibit. *Kenner Historical Museum,* 1922 Third, is housed in the former residence of long-time Jefferson Parish Sheriff Frank Clancy. It features memorabilia and artifacts of Kenner agricultural and historical significance, a Black History room, and other exhibits. The *New Orleans Saints Museum and Hall of Fame,* 409 Williams, exhibits uniforms, photos, and memorabilia of the local professional football team. *Freeport-McMoRan Science Center, Planetarium and Observatory* features hands-on exhibits and programs related to science and astronomy. *LaSalle's Landing,* Williams and Third Street, is a Mississippi River overlook and landscaped plaza.

JEFFERSON PARISH, WEST BANK: David Crockett Fire Hall, 205 Lafayette, Gretna, was completed in 1859. It houses the Gould No. 31 Steam Fire Pumper, purchased in 1876, the only steam fire engine of its kind still in existence. Open daily. (504-366-4491). **Magnolia Lane Plantation,** River Road (La. 541), Westwego, was built in 1784 in West Indies style. It stands on what was the Old Spanish Trail, the only wagon road from the west to New Orleans. By appt. Admission. (504-347-1323)

To continue south of New Orleans, please refer to page 159.

SALVADOR WILDLIFE MANAGEMENT AREA: located along the northwest shore of Lake Salvador, this 31,000-acre, primarily freshwater marsh tract is accessible by boat and offers hunting, trapping by permit, excellent fishing, nature study, boating, and picnicking. (504-568-5885)

DES ALLEMANDS: literally, "the Germans" in French, U.S. 90, was settled by German immigrants over 250 years ago, as were several other towns in this area known as the German Coast. **Louisiana Catfish Festival,** held the second weekend in July, features championship road race, catfish skinning contest, beauty pageant, entertainment, and food. (504-758-7542)

THE GREAT RIVER ROAD: there are two roads along the Mississippi River, one following the levee along each side. Both are narrow, scenic, and pass a variety of plantation homes, 18th-century Creole cottages, vintage commercial buildings, churches and churchyards, and tiny, rural communities. The Great River Road on the west side is La. 18; on the east side, La. 44 and 628. The best way to meander the River Road is with detailed tourist information as many of the area buildings and sites are either private or need explanations. Tourist information: St. James Parish (504-869-9752), St. John the Baptist Parish (504-652-9569), St. Charles Parish (504-783-5140). (To continue north on the River Road, see Chapter 6, Baton Rouge and its environs.)

ST. ROSE: La Branche Dependency House, built circa 1792, is the bachelor quarters and only remaining structure of a sugar plantation on this site. An oak alley enhances the beauty of the property. Tours daily except holidays, 10-4. Admission. (504-468-8843)

LULING: U.S. 90, on the west side of the Mississippi River, is the site of the St. Charles Parish Planetarium, housed in the St. Charles Parish West Branch Library at Lakewood. It features changing planetarium shows on Saturdays and Monday and Wednesday nights. Also telescope viewing. (504-785-8471). **Cochon de Lait Festival,** held the first weekend in November, features a parade, dance, food, auction, and entertainment.

BONNET CARRÉ SPILLWAY: built in the early 1930s as an emergency floodway to divert water from the Mississippi River to Lake Pontchartrain in case of the threat of high water to New Orleans, the tract, managed by the Army Corps of Engineers, is hardwood and grassy marsh, offering fishing, boat launching, and tent camping.

DESTREHAN: on La. 48, adjacent to the Hale Boggs Bridge

(I-310), is **Destrehan Plantation,** built in 1787. It is a former indigo plantation and one of the oldest plantation homes left intact in the lower Mississippi Valley. Very early construction methods were discovered during restoration and are shown. Open daily except holidays, 9-4. Admission. (504-764-9315). **Destrehan Fall Festival,** held on the grounds of the plantation house, features crafts, food, and entertainment. **Spring Festival of the Arts,** held the first weekend in May, features arts, crafts, and entertainment. Admission. **Ormond Plantation** on River Road, built circa 1790, is in the Spanish colonial style. Tours daily except holidays, 10-4:30. Admission. (504-764-8544). **St. Charles Borromeo Catholic Church** complex features a cemetery with headstones dating from the 18th century and the "Little Red Church," used from 1806 to 1922. **Home Place Plantation,** built in 1790, is a singular example of West Indies-style architecture. By appt. (504-783-2123)

MANCHAC AREA: At I-55/U.S. 51 exit 22, **Joyce Wildlife Management Area** features a 1,000-foot swamp boardwalk and nature trail into one of the largest uninhabited swamps of Louisiana. **Manchac,** a tiny fishing village located on a strip of land between Lakes Maurepas and Pontchartrain, offers swamp tours, boat launches, and good fishing areas. **Manchac Wildlife Management Area,** the 8,300-acre tract of swampland between Lakes Maurepas and Pontchartrain, is accessible by boat. Hunting, trapping, alligator trapping by permit, fishing, and crabbing. (504-324-5875)

RESERVE: **San Francisco plantation**, built in 1856 with a Creole floor plan in Steamboat Gothic style, features five ceiling frescoes. Open daily except holidays, 10-4. (504-535-2341)

EDGARD: The St. John the Baptist Church and Cemetery date from 1770, with tombs from the early 19th century. The Edgard-Reserve Mississippi River ferry landing is located across the River Road from the church. **Evergreen Plantation**, La. 18 west of Edgard, is a Greek Revival-style home with curved outer staircase built in the 1820s, still part of a working sugar plantation. Drive-by.

GARYVILLE: **Timbermill Museum**, Main at Railroad, is housed in a restored lumber mill circa 1903 and features exhibits of River Road culture and the timber industry. Call for hours. (504-535-3202). San Francisco Plantation, on River Road, built in 1854 in the old Creole floor plan, has only a dining room and service rooms on the ground floor. Five ceiling frescoes grace the interior; the exterior is Steamboat Gothic. Open daily except holidays, 10-4. Admission. (504-535-2341)

GRAMERCY: Lutcher and Gramercy are abutting towns on the east side of the Mississippi River, sharing a street that acts as a town boundary. Gramercy bills itself as the Bonfire Capital of the World and hosts numerous bonfires on the levee on Christmas Eve. (see essay).

LUTCHER: east landing, Lutcher-Vacherie ferry. **Perique tobacco** grows only in St. James Parish. The native plant has a big, very thick leaf, which dries to make extremely strong tobacco. It is no longer made into cigarettes and is only used in a mixed pipe blend made in England. Only a few farmers still grow perique, which the French settlers learned to cultivate from the Indians. Farm and barn tours June and July by appt. (504-869-3098)

VACHERIE: (pronounced "vash-eree"). **Oak Alley Plantation,** built 1837-39, is a fine example of Greek Revival architecture, but is especially known for its alley of 28 evenly spaced live oaks, thought to be at least 100 years older than the big house. A slave on the plantation during the 1840s is credited with the creation of over 100 species of pecan trees. The house is open daily, Mar.-Oct., 9-5:30; Nov.-Feb., 9-5. Closed holidays. Admission. (504-265-2151). **A Christmas bonfire party** features jazz, choirs, food, and a bonfire on the levee, held the second Saturday in December. Admission.

ST. JAMES: La. 18, is the site of **St. James Catholic Church,** constructed in the 19th century, containing the original furnishings and ancient oil paintings of the stations of the cross presented to the church by Valcour Aimé. **St. James Cemetery,** on the site of the first Acadian settlements in Louisiana in 1756, is one of the oldest cemeteries in the state and contains graves of prominent parish families. **Bonfires on the levee** line both sides of the Mississippi River in St. James Parish on Christmas Eve.

CONVENT: La. 44. Manresa House of Retreats, built in 1831 in the Gothic Revival-style to house Jefferson College, now serves as the center of a Jesuit retreat compound for laymen. If the gates are open, no retreat is going on and visitors may come in and stroll the grounds. **St. Michael's Catholic Church** was built in 1809 in the Gothic style to save east bank residents from having to cross the river to attend services. It contains a replica of France's Lourdes grotto constructed of bagasse, a byproduct in the processing of sugarcane. The hand-carved altar came from the Paris Exposition of 1867. The old cemetery cemetery contains interesting tombs. **Judge Poche Plantation,** built in 1870 in the Victorian Renaissance revival style, has been beautifully restored and furnished. By appt. Admission. (504-562-3537)

SOUTH OF NEW ORLEANS: The area south and southeast of New Orleans becomes a low, flat land of swamp and marsh except along the river and bayous where high ground has built up. It is an historic area of natural beauty, sprinkled with historic houses and buildings, offering excellent fishing, hunting, and bird-watching. The oil and oil service industries and maritime-related businesses maintain an important presence.

BAYOU SEGNETTE STATE PARK: off the Westbank Expressway (U.S. 90B) in Westwego, is a 600-acre scenic wetlands wilderness area, including a small lake and bayous, accessible from U.S. 90. Offers canoeing, boating, bird-watching, hiking trail, fishing, camping, and cabins. Handicapped access. Admission. (504-436-1107)

LAFITTE: Jean Lafitte National Historical Park, Barataria Unit, west of La. 45, is an 8,600-acre preserve of coastal wetlands, including freshwater marsh, swamps, and hardwood forests. A museum and interpretive center feature exhibits on hunting, trapping, fishing, and early lifestyles. Open daily, 9-5. Best access to the wetlands is to explore by canoe. Guided canoe tours by National Park Service rangers on Sundays. (504-589-2330)

(The most southerly point of Jefferson Parish, Grand Isle, can be reached by land only via La. 1. See Chapter 7, Houma/Thibodaux and the South Central.)

CHALMETTE: The St. Bernard Parish Historical Society offers information and tours. (504-279-9401). The town hosts the **Tomato Festival,** with pageants, food, entertainment. **Jean Lafitte National Historical Park, Chalmette Unit,** La. 46, is the historic battleground where the Battle of New Orleans was fought in the War of 1812, January 15, 1815, between Gen. Andrew Jackson's forces and British troops under Gen. Edward Pakenham. The park includes a reconstruction of Jackson's rampart, a tour road of important points on the battlefield, and exhibits and interpretive program housed in the Beauregard House Visitor Center. Open daily, 8:30-5. (504-589-4428). The Chalmette National Cemetery is also on the property. Picnicking. A reenactment of the battle is held each year in January. **De La Ronde Oaks,** La.46, planted in 1762, extend from the roadside ruins of the old Versailles plantation back to the river.

ST. BERNARD: La. 46, established in 1780 as San Bernardo, the last bastion of Spanish colonial culture in Louisiana. **Jean Lafitte National Historical Park, Islenos Museum,** exhibits and explicates the history and culture of the Canary Islanders who settled in St. Bernard Parish between 1779 and 1783. Vintage photos, arts, crafts, tools, and other memorabilia housed in a cottage dating from 1750. Open daily, 8:30-5. (504-682-0862). **Ducros Museum,** La. 46, housed in an early Creole cottage built in 1800, exhibits artifacts and memorablia significant in the history of St. Bernard. Open weekdays, 10-5; Sat., 10-4. (504-682-2713). **St. Bernard State Park,** La. 39, a 358-acre property with manmade lagoons, nature trails, fishing, boating, and camping.

Public transportation 1/2 mile away. (504-682-2101). **Museum Days,** held at the two museums, include guided tours, demonstrations of heritage crafts by local craftsmen.

TOCA: Terre-aux-Boeufs Cemetery, La. 46, one of the oldest burial grounds in Louisiana, with the first recorded interment in 1787. The family of Gen. P. G. T. Beauregard is buried here.

BRAITHWAITE: La. 39 on the east bank of Plaquemines Parish, **Mary Plantation,** built in the late 18th century in the Santo Domingo style of West Indies architecture. By appt. (504-564-2761)

BELLE CHASSE: site of Alvin Callender Naval Air Station, a national defense site. **The Mississippi River ferry** crosses the river between here and Braithwaite.

BILOXI WILDLIFE MANAGEMENT AREA: a 40,000-acre tract of coastal marsh, accessible by water, offers hunting, fishing, shrimping, bird-watching, boating, camping.

LAKE HERMITAGE: formerly Lake Judge Perez, located off La. 23, 5 miles south of Myrtle Grove, and 5 miles west on gravel road. Scenic road—one of the most picturesque areas, including swamp, marsh, and high ground with moss-draped trees and lazy waterways. A small fishing village and boat dock are at the lake.

WEST POINTE A LA HACHE: the regularly scheduled Mississippi River ferry, crossing to Pointe a la Hache, offers excellent views of the river and oceangoing ships. At Pointe a la Hache, the **Plaquemines Parish Tourist Commission,** located in the historic parish courthouse, offers information, maps, and brochures. (504-564-2761)

EMPIRE: La. 23, "Seafood Capital of Plaquemines Parish," is a base for deep sea fishing and charter boats. **Empire/South Pass Tarpon Rodeo,** held the third weekend in August. All fish entered during the rodeo are displayed at the official weighing station. Fees. (504-657-9811)

BURAS: La. 23, Louisiana's citrus-producing center, with groves planted in the narrow strip of high ground along the Mississippi River because the land falls away rapidly into marsh and wooded swamp.

FORT JACKSON: La. 23, between Triumph and Boothville, is an 82-acre property on which stands the restored massive, star-shaped fort, built in 1822-32, to protect New Orleans and the lower river. It withstood a 10-day seige by the Union Navy in 1862 only to surrender after New Orleans fell. A small museum of war relics, camp ground, and picnicking. Open daily, 7-7. Museum open weekdays, 10-4; weekends, 11-5. (504-657-7083). **La Salle monument,** next to Fort Jackson on a manmade reservoir, commemorates the discovery of Louisiana in 1682 by French explorer Robert Cavelier, Sieur de La Salle. **Plaquemines Parish Fair and Orange Festival,** held the first weekend in

December, offers food, entertainment, exhibits, catfish skinning and cleaning contest, duck calling, fais-do-do, and citrus. (504-656-7752). **Fourth of July Festival,** held the second weekend in August, features games, entertainment, pirogue races in the lake. **Fort St. Phillip,** a companion fort constructed in 1795, is visible across the Mississippi River but is not open to the public.

VENICE: nicknamed "the Jump," is the end point of La. 23, departure point for charter fishing boats into the Gulf of Mexico, and hub for the oil service industry. **Delta National Wildlife Refuge,** a 70,000-acre tract, offers protection for a variety of migratory birds and wildlife. Sport hunting, fishing and shrimping with permits. Accessible by boat. **Deep Delta River Excursions,** boat tours to the Delta National Wildlife Refuge, Pilot Town, Burrwood, Ft. Eads lighthouse, and the Gulf of Mexico available. Admission. (504-392-6690 or 504-564-2925)

PILOT TOWN: tiny community, accessible only by boat, near the top of the Mississippi River delta, where the river pilots and bar pilots are headquartered.

PASS A LOUTRE WILDLIFE MANAGEMENT AREA: a 66,000-acre tract of floating marsh at the mouth of the Mississippi River, offers hunting, trapping by permit, fishing, boating, camping along the river levee. Accessible by boat only. (504-568-5885)

BRETON NATIONAL WILDLIFE REFUGE: in the Chandeleur Sound of the Gulf of Mexico, a chain of offshore barrier islands that is a shorebird, gull, and tern nesting area. Fishing permitted during daylight hours. No camping. Accessible by boat.

MISSISSIPPI RIVER GULF OUTLET CANAL: runs from the Gulf of Mexico, south of St. Bernard Parish, on a straight diagonal past Yscloskey to join the Intracoastal Waterway just east of New Orleans. This manmade waterway provides more direct access to the port of New Orleans from the east, cutting time from the 9-hour trip from the mouth of the river to New Orleans.

Unique Louisiana

PILOT TOWN

On an eroding triangle island carved from the marsh, just north of where Southwest Pass, South Pass, and Pass a Loutre meet like the fingers of a splayed hand, is the watery outpost called Pilot Town, an edge of civilization with a gritty charisma all its own. Here, at the slip end of a nearly 4,000-mile superhighway, is a string of ramshackle buildings and walkways that comprises the last populated settlement along the Mississippi River.

Pilot Town was so named because the bar pilots and the river pilots, who trade duties at this latitude out in the middle of the vast river, have been headquartered here since 1880. The river pilots debark after trips south from New Orleans, or before taking a ship north to the Crescent City; the bar pilots await orders to maneuver their trust down to the Gulf of Mexico's landmark navigational buoy, or rest up here after bringing one of the behemoths from open water through the shifting channels up to this point. Any on-duty pilot who isn't on the water is hanging around Pilot Town.

In its heyday, as many as 350 people lived here—families with children, trappers, and fishermen, in addition to the cyclically arriving pilots. But today, only a handful of the older generation still resides in this world apart, where boats provide the only access. It is a male-dominated order, operating around the activities and support systems for the men who are pilots.

Seen from the river, Pilot Town is a spindly necklace of buildings on stilts, draped between the marsh and the swirling, brown water. Its main street, and only thoroughfare, is a three-quarter-mile-long concrete walkway—a mere six feet wide, sufficient as a promenade for pedestrians or a causeway for bicyclists but too narrow for cars. But, then, there are no cars in Pilot Town. The artery runs from the willow-lined wilderness on one end of the community to the two-tank oil depot on the other. The previous main drag was a wooden boardwalk and a mud levee that succumbed to hurricanes.

Though "Main Street" was rebuilt, the heart of Pilot Town's commercial district was blown apart by a devil-woman named Camille. In its heyday, the district consisted of a grocery store and two bars, which serviced both residents and a flurry of visitors who ferried in off the river. The post office, Zip Code 70081, survives, however. During the morning mail sort, the postal trailer is a throbbing social hub. Across the way, the one-room schoolhouse has been transformed into a private residence. It withstood the hurricane, but not the subsequent emigration of young people.

Modest wooden homes, like fishing camps or beach houses, connect to the main street by wooden walks on stilts. Cisterns and abandoned boat hulls collect rainwater. The occasional garden warily grows on a high patch of ground that might be swept away any time by high water. Anyone's back door panorama is the same—either the river or the marsh, depending on which side of the causeway it's on.

The side-by-side white boardinghouses of the pilots dominate the island. The bar pilots' rambling, two-story, clapboard house, originally erected in 1918, is nicely remodeled inside to resemble a fraternity house after inspection. The river pilots, next door in a sprawling, West Indian-style landmark, share the front yard of natural lawn and weathered boardwalks that lead to the marina, the equivalent of Pilot Town's town square. Its docks and jetties reach into the muddy flow of the river, welcoming and dispatching pilot boats and service craft, runabouts, suppliers, and deliverers of news and mail.

Except for an occasional fisherman, few visitors look for Pilot Town. It's too remote, linked to no public transportation, and has nothing to see if you go. It's merely the epicenter of a *sui generis* industry where the real work happens elsewhere . . . an edge of civilization hanging on tight in the changing delta, in the changing world, on the mighty Mississippi.

ST. CHARLES AVENUE STREETCAR

A barreling, fume-spewing bus may be speedier and more efficient, but the St. Charles Avenue Streetcar is a far more charming and interesting way to travel about New Orleans. As it creaks and jangles, rattles and sways along polished metal rails, under green archways of heavy-limbed oaks, it passes gracious nineteenth-century mansions with elegant, leaded-glass doors, vintage neoclassical offices frosted with terra-cotta, and the higgledy-piggledy tangle of residence and commerce, old and new, engaging and needy, that, like the streetcar, is the essence of this remarkable city.

The St. Charles Avenue Streetcar is a two-layered treasure. Preservationists celebrate its title as the oldest continuously operating streetcar line in the world, now listed on the National Register of Historic Places. It has provided service along this busy and fashionable thoroughfare since 1835 with a parade of the most up-to-date equipment including double-decker, mule-drawn trolleys, "man-powered" trolleys (once, when the horses were too sick to work), steam-powered engines, and the new-fangled, still-used "electrified cars." Where a network of fifty street railways once crisscrossed the city, the St. Charles Streetcar is now the sole survivor with heritage.

But, to locals, "riding the streetcar" isn't the line so much as it is climbing aboard one of the remaining stock of thirty-five snub-nosed, military green, friendly-faced Perley Thomas motorcars that have been in use since 1923-24. Despite the addition of computerized fare boxes that beep and new paint and varnish that shine, the St. Charles Avenue Streetcar is a relic of another era, a jolly combination of efficiency and amusement.

There's a special invitation to ride when, at each station stop, the double-panelled doors part and the steps unfold, revealing the motorman, enthroned on a pedestaled seat. His stature is enhanced by the black curtains, half-encasing the cockpit where he operates the antique apparatus for stop and go, open and close, with commanding

St. Charles Avenue streetcar. (Courtesy Louisiana Office of Tourism)

presence. Once upon a time, his mirror-image, the conductor, reigned in an identical setting at the rear.

Long wooden benches run lengthwise along the front and rear of the car. The rest of the lucky passengers crunch into eight pairs of crosswise wooden seats with backs that slide forward, to make a party booth for two intimate couples. The wood glows with a rich patina, as warm as a Royal Street antique, from the inadvertent polishing of generations of seated riders. Even the triangular brass grips at the corner of each seatback glow with high gloss from decades of standing passengers clutching security as the car careens along the tracks.

With its vaulted ceiling and studded metal carapace, the streetcar makes a cozy capsule, humming and clanking, welcoming men in straw hats and white linen suits, discharging ladies with flowered handkerchiefs and bulging shopping bags, exchanging book-bag-backed students for riders in uniforms of every description. In warm weather, passengers raise the square windows, hanging their elbows and arms outside to create a colorful linear abstract along the green exterior.

As the car churns along its route, the motorman jangles his bell with the imperious insistence of an airhorn, warning unwary motorists and pedestrians, joggers and eighteen-wheelers, to clear the way. The streetcar's kingdom is defined by two metal rails laid through the heart of the city. The motorman's trust is a treasure: the St. Charles Avenue Streetcar, insouciant dowager queen of everyman's New Orleans.

Unique Louisiana

BONFIRES ON THE LEVEE

Christmas Eve in south Louisiana may be balmy or bone-chilling but along the River Road between Gramercy/Lutcher and the Sunshine Bridge, Christmas Eve is always a hot time.

It's the night of Bonfires on the Levee, one of the most unusual annual festivals on the state's crowded festival calendar. The spectacle is mesmerizing—a seemingly infinite line of log pyramids constructed along the spine of the Mississippi River levee, simultaneously set ablaze to create a dazzling row of brass and orange flame curtains fluttering against a soft, dark sky, blasting gold sparks into the night air.

Once upon a time, the evening was a small, local celebration for families and friends who waited for Papa Noel (the Cajun version of Santa Claus) to arrive along the River. It has evolved into an Event, a swarm of partying visitors on foot and creeping lines of traffic clogging River Road until nearly midnight.

Explanations of the Bonfires' origin abound: it is a Cajun bayou custom to light Papa Noel's way; the French Catholics, for whom Christmas Eve is a religious occasion, needed bonfires to help them find their way in the dark to midnight mass; the bonfires began, not on the night before Christmas, but on New Year's Eve or Twelfth Night (January 6), customary present-exchange nights. The more historically oriented suggest bonfire lighting was an old French custom brought over by the Marist priests who came to teach at nearby Jefferson College (now the Manresa House of Retreats in Convent). Regardless of its origins, the Christmas Eve celebration on the St. James Parish levee has become an unusual scene.

Longtime residents of the River Road remember bonfire-building as a children's activity between Thanksgiving and Christmas. Boys and girls would spend days finding and cutting young willows from the batture (the land between the levee and the river), amassing an impressive collection of cane reeds, bamboo, logs, and old tires, and amassing an impressive pile. On Christmas Eve, local families would visit, eat and drink, and burn up the gathered material. Often, a log pyramid was erected to make a better bonfire.

It was a quiet, local celebration until the 1970s when the local volunteer firemen turned the evening a bit more public by offering some low-profile hospitality to the gaggle of visitors who had heard about this colorful ritual. Word of mouth had a snowball effect on public attendance and, as increasing numbers of visitors came, more local families began building bonfires on the levee.

Some oldtimers say they regret the changes—the traffic, the crowds, the firecrackers, the tootling paddlewheelers on the river, and the buzzing helicopters in the air from TV news crews and state police. It's no longer a quiet evening, but a well-orchestrated event, beginning with the regulated letting of nearly a hundred bonfire-building permits, which strictly stipulate the placement and shape of bonfire structures—150 feet apart, pyramid-log cabin style, only a certain height and size. Tires are now prohibited—they pollute—and the batture is no longer fair game for wood. And, of course, the volunteer firemen sell jambalaya and gumbo dinners to a never-ending line of hungry visitors as well as logo-typed sweatshirts, and bonfire beer mugs. Moreover, they have a permit to build an extravagant bonfire structure—a viking ship, a plantation house, a three-car train, or some other large, fancy creation—which they light at the same time the Fire Chief gives his signal for all bonfires to burn.

Like every south Louisiana festival, Bonfires on the Levee is a party, an excuse to have a good time. And if burning down painstaking constructions seems an odd centerpiece for a celebration, so be it. But the spectacle of the fires is beautiful, carefully regulated, and filled with joie de vivre and Christmas spirit—a toast to Papa Noel. Only in south Louisiana!

If Midnight mass didn't exist to kill the evening, it would have to be invented.

Index

174   GUIDE TO LOUISIANA